EMBRACING LIFE FROM DEATH

A Caregiver's Journey through Glioblastoma, Grief, and Healing

Anitra Marie Simmons

Publishing services provided by **Archangel Ink**

ISBN-13: 978-1-9791-1133-1

YOUR FREE GUIDE

Before you begin reading this book, I have a free bonus to offer you.

In addition to the information already provided in this book, I have created a printable one-page PDF with 10 things every caregiver of glioblastoma needs to know.

To receive your free printable, sign up for the my mailing list by visiting http://embracinglifefromdeath.blogspot.com

Signing up will also notify you of any pending book releases or updated content. By subscribing you will be first in line for exclusive deals and future book giveaways.

Immediately after signing up you'll be sent an email with access to the bonus.

–Anitra

CONTENTS

PROLOGUE

"In sickness and in health, till death do us part …"

Every married couple speaks these vows, or some version of them, but few of us think about the reality attached to them. How can we? The hope, joy, and bliss of a wedding are too wonderful to be tainted by all the possibilities of how your bright future together can go wrong.

But none of us are promised a fairytale ending. That's exactly why we make these promises. Because we will inevitably suffer. We will walk through sickness. And one day, death will part us.

On the day I made these vows to the love of my life, Dean, I had no idea what it would mean to uphold them twelve years later. I was too enthralled with the bliss of having found a good man, so unlike the other men in my past.

My first love was an abusive, violent young man named George. I was very naïve at the age of sixteen, and ripe to a manipulative and angry boy, who was nineteen when we met. Three years was a huge difference in maturity at that age, but I was strong-willed and ready for attention from a male figure, even if it was the wrong kind. I had misgivings but didn't know what to do. He had raped me and taken my virginity, and I had been taught I was damaged from having sex before I was married. Being raised Catholic, I was very aware that premarital sex was bad behavior. Because of that, I felt worthless to any other man and believed I had to marry him.

As time went on, George became much more mentally and physically abusive. It wasn't until he started to beat me that I woke up from the spell he had on me. One night he came home drunk, screaming filthy names at me and beating me. I decided that I was going to leave and never come back.

I had one friend at that time in my life, a coworker named John who had supported me through my relationship with George and would make me laugh; he also helped to keep my fears and anxiety at bay. During my breakup with George, my relationship with John grew. For the first time, I was protected and loved by a nice man. I did not stop to think that maybe I needed time to grow up and really decide what I wanted out of life. I went full steam ahead, and before I knew it, John and I were engaged. I was still only nineteen years old, but I had a fiancé and was planning my wedding.

By the time I was twenty, I was already married to my best friend, John, and was pregnant with our first child, Tia. I never stopped long enough to ask myself what I was doing with my life. I let life happen to me, rather than plan it out. I was happy to be with John; I felt safe and in love.

One of the first signs early in our relationship that alerted me something wasn't right, was when John told me that since I was no longer a virgin, he wasn't sure he wanted to marry me. I swallowed my apprehension, secretly agreeing with him that I was still damaged goods and hoping I was worthy enough that he would not break up with me. John also had a very violent temper. He would throw objects or punch holes in walls when he was upset. Another sign I ignored was when he told me if I ever cheated, he would kill me.

I became pregnant with Hannah when I turned twenty-five, already having inklings of discontentment with my life and thinking that having another child would make it better. But as time went on, my desire to live differently and do the things I wanted became stronger. I still loved John, but I was no longer "in love" with him.

Eventually, I asked my husband for a divorce after having a secret affair with a coworker, Jack. When John found out about the affair, he became physically abusive, as he had promised. All of the feelings from my first relationship flooded back into my brain and my body at that moment. My worst fears had come true, and my husband, who I had once thought was safe, had hurt me. He was always a good father and provider, but I felt my affair caused our marriage to end with anger and violence.

Ultimately, I carried the shame and blame for the demise of my marriage. Soon after, we divorced and that chapter of my life was over. I was ready to move on. With the help of a therapist, I came to terms with my poor decisions. I learned that Jack, the man I had the affair with, was a master manipulator. I thought I had been in love with him, but realized I was the victim, and that I was never going to win. I had to let it go. It was a painful process, and it took over three years for me to create a new normal. But when I finally did, I met Dean.

PART ONE

MY JOURNEY BEGINS

Dean and I met for lunch one blustery, cold day following a huge windstorm that had recently knocked power out to thousands of people all over the Seattle area. It was early winter, and I had recently purchased a home in a new neighborhood in Maple Valley, Washington. My life had changed drastically over the last three years, but I was finally ready to start a relationship and live a happier life. I had been divorced, left my job with a drilling contractor, and started an exciting position in a new company as a finance manager for a local builder. It was 2003, and the building industry was on the cusp of a real estate explosion. My new job was challenging, different from what I had done in the past, and very busy. I loved it!

Both Dean and I had been married before; he had been single for nine years, and I for over three. He chose me through a dating service called Great Expectations, which we were both members of. I had been dating long enough to have low expectations (not great) about what was, essentially, blind dating. He was a project manager for a large dock company in Seattle, and he frequently worked in the San Juan Islands managing waterfront projects. The first time he called me on my cell phone, I was walking up and down Second Ave with a girlfriend in downtown Seattle, blindly looking for a place to eat dinner.

"Hello?" Dean said. I was instantly charmed by his low sexy voice, even though I was distracted by my friend while she read menus posted outside the restaurant doors.

"Hi, this is Anitra. Who is this?" I asked breathlessly, trying to keep pace with my friend.

"This is Dean Simmons, from Great Expectations. How you doin'?" he said in his husky voice.

"Is that supposed to be Joey on *Friends*?" I joked back.

"Why yes ... yes, it is ..." he laughed.

"So, what are you doing?" I asked him next, not knowing what to say.

"Well, I'm sitting in my truck, in the San Juan Islands, waiting for a ferry while getting up the nerve to call you. I would love to take you out and get to know you. I had to call the sales director to get your number. Seems once I asked you out, the dating service system wouldn't give your phone number again. Since I requested to meet you a year ago, I had to get special help to contact you."

"Wow, all that to meet me?" I paused a moment for dramatic effect. "I have to confess, your director called me and had to get my permission to let you contact me. I had to ask her what you looked like and if you were nice. Even though I already accepted your request a year ago, I couldn't remember anything about you. She could not say enough good things about you ... she went on and on about how cute, funny, and nice you are ... made me wonder if she wanted to date you herself," I joked.

He laughed. "If you saw her, you would see that she is a very nice *older* lady. Not for me—but a great person. So … would you like to meet for lunch next week?"

"I would love to. Let's meet at a small brewery in Issaquah off Main Street at noon on Thursday. Does that work?" I asked.

"I look forward to it. See you then," he replied.

Later that week, when I walked into the Issaquah Brewhouse, I noticed him at a table, looking up through his reader glasses at me. I nodded to him, and he gazed back at me with a little smile to acknowledge that he was waiting for me. Dean had a striking resemblance to the country singer Alan Jackson—tall and handsome with soft blond hair that curled at the neckline. I remember he did not order food for lunch, and I thought that a little odd and annoying, as I don't like to eat alone. But he was funny and nice, and I liked him okay. We talked for a while and then left the restaurant. He walked me to my car, I gave him a hug, and we agreed to get together again soon. Later, we laughed when he told me he thought I was opinionated and outspoken, and I told him I thought he was a little old and stodgy.

It didn't take long for me to learn that Dean had a quiet, gentle presence about him, mixed with a bawdy sense of humor. He was an avid outdoorsman who loved to fish, hunt, and garden. He was strong, yet sensitive, and he always made me laugh. As I got to know him, I could not believe I was so lucky to find this hidden gem in the pool of bachelors I had previously gone out with. Everyone loved Dean—he was so engaging and witty that he made friends wherever he went. He swept me off my feet in no time, and we quickly fell in love. He was so handsome, and he had this dry sense of humor that constantly cracked me up. I always felt beautiful around him, and he treated me like a princess.

In the twelve years we had together, that never changed. We were both broken from our previous relationships, and it was like coming home when we found each other. Getting to know and date Dean was one of the most exciting times in my life. As I started to fall deeply in love with him, my happiness rose exponentially. Every date night felt like I was going to prom. I would excitedly get dressed up, anticipating the evening ahead. We met all over the Seattle area, trying different restaurants, going to movies we never would have seen before meeting each other, and attending Broadway shows, plays, and concerts. I loved that he was always up for anything I wanted to do, no matter how crazy. He was the most spontaneous man I had ever met. Going out for dinner and drinks, combined with our physical chemistry, was so romantic that sometimes we wouldn't make it home before ending up making love in the front seat of my truck. Now that was crazy for me, a mother of two at forty years old.

For the first time since I could remember, I was truly happy. I did not want to run away, hide, or quit my life as I had so many times before. Soon, it felt like Dean and I had been a couple forever, our lives quickly intertwining in every aspect.

Dean moved in with me after a year of dating. He romantically proposed after six more months, surprising me with a beautiful platinum diamond ring. We had driven from Seattle to Montana, destination Cameron, where we had reservations at Papoose Creek Lodge. This was our first big trip together, and we even stopped at the Silverwood Theme Park in Idaho on the way. We rode the roller coasters, ate junk food, and played theme park games. One day later, we arrived at the lodge, a large, imposing log cabin structure that only had limited guests at one time. The rooms inside were like huge bedrooms in a rustic mansion. They featured thick down comforters, rustic furniture, and decadent bathrooms. The lodge also offered a private chef for every meal, and the food and wine were amazing. We were close to the Madison River, where Dean and I wanted to go fly-fishing, and there were stables for horseback riding for both of us. He was nervous and proposed almost upon our arrival, after I had showered and was lying down to take a nap. As he leaned over me, asking me to share our lives together, I laughed to myself, thinking, *He's really doing this now? While I have a towel on my head and nothing on but a robe?*

Of course, I said yes, and we kissed, hugged, and snuggled, realizing our lives were going to change forever. Later, we told the other guests at dinner, and they bought champagne for all of us to celebrate. The whole week was amazing, and I will never forget it.

We married on January 6, 2006, a little over two years after we met. Our wedding started out to be very small—just us and our daughters. I had two daughters from my first marriage, Hannah and Tia, and Dean had a daughter named Karly from his first marriage. Karly was one year younger than Hannah and blended right in with our little family. But I wanted my sister, Lisa, to be at my side when I married, and Dean wanted his best friend, Jim, as his best man. We had decided to marry at the courthouse instead of having a traditional wedding. So, eventually, our little intimate party ended up being thirteen of us: our daughters and my parents, sister, and brother-in-law; Tia's boyfriend; my friend Marie; and Jim and his wife. The girls and I spent the day getting our nails done and getting dressed up while Dean transformed into my handsome prince in his black suit and tie.

Lisa became the unofficial photographer, and took pictures outside the courthouse steps. The party ended up at Daniel's Broiler on Union Harbor for dinner. They offered us a private room, and we all sat at one big table, drinking, toasting, and laughing. The room and service were amazing; it was intimate, cozy, and loving. From there, all the guests followed us to the Edgewater Inn on the Seattle waterfront. Dean and I had a suite on the water for the night and had gotten the girls a room nearby. We shared cake and opened gifts from our loved ones. Soon, everyone went home, and we kicked the girls off our bed and sent them to their own room.

Life continued moving fast, and we were so happy. There were the usual adjustments when melding families and balancing work and play, but we'd managed to build our dream house the prior year, moving in by February, one month after our wedding, and going to Italy in June 2006 for our honeymoon for two weeks. Dean used to introduce me to old friends and acquaintances, not only as his wife, but saying I should have been his first wife. He was so proud of me, and I of him. We continued to do everything together. We took trips for hiking and fly-fishing, had regular date nights for dinner and movies, and went to concerts and traveled. We would pick different destinations every year and take turns on who got to choose. I usually went with his choice, as I loved to make him happy. I'm very glad I agreed to his destinations, as he was able to cross a lot of places and things he wanted to do off his bucket list.

We cherished each other in an appreciative way, as we were both on our second marriage and realized how special this union was. Dean used to say that he didn't deserve me, our home, and his life. It was too good to be true. I would remind him that we both worked hard for our accomplishments and deserved each other and everything we worked for together, including our family.

When the economy fell in 2007, we decided to reinvent ourselves. Dean was tired of all the driving he had to do for his project manager job, and I was losing my position as head of finance and project manager for a builder. I had been prepping Dean for months to get him to start a company with me, as I hated his absence when he traveled to the San Juan Islands for work. He finally took the plunge in February of 2007, and we dedicated ourselves to building an exterior contracting business. He had the technical skill, and I had the business and financial experience. Together we made a wonderful team. Balancing each other out with our strengths, we worked seven days a week to build and grow our little business. When we were awarded projects, we celebrated ecstatically and took so much pleasure in reaping the rewards of our hard labor.

Dean was a workaholic by nature, and I continued to bug him about finding a balance of pleasure and business. With us running our own company, it was easy for him to sink into working nonstop and not separate business from personal life. I worried about the stress he put on himself and always asked him to slow down and find time for himself. I constantly worried about his health, making sure he was eating right and exercising.

Dean and I had so much love for each other. Every night after dinner, we would watch movies in bed while holding hands. We would talk about events of the day and crack each other up with jokes. We laughed so much that it was my favorite time of day. Even when we had the occasional fight, it never lasted long. We both felt lost without the other and couldn't stand not speaking for long. As time went on, our love grew deeper. It was rare that we spent a night apart, and running our business together required that we speak many times throughout the day. We became inseparable.

Our idyllic life continued as we spent time traveling two to three times a year. We loved to upgrade and work on our property and spend time with family and friends. Most recently, we had been turning our backyard into a beautiful oasis, adding a waterfall and cobblestone patio. Dean built a large rustic cedar structure that looked like the covered picnic areas at the park, next to the waterfall. I added an outdoor carpet with rattan couch, ottoman, and cushions for comfortable outdoor living, and we started adding a large deck with a pool and hot tub. He was so proud of the backyard and gardens. He could work all day but come home and spend hours outside, weeding, raking, or planting flowers. I would ask him why he didn't relax more, and he would always say that working in the garden was his relaxation.

As our lives unfolded together, time passed quickly, and our love continued to grow deeper. After forty years, I had finally found contentment in my life.

DISCOVERING SOMETHING WRONG

June 27, 2015

I looked around the dining room, waiting for our breakfast to be served and wondered why I felt so on edge. We still had twenty-four hours left in our beautiful room overlooking the harbor at the Delta Victoria Ocean Point Resort, and it was a lovely warm day in Victoria, BC.

At the sound of Dean's voice, I turned my attention back to him.

"I want to go home," he announced.

I realized that was exactly what I'd been feeling, and I nodded my head in agreement. "Me too." I said.

"Are you feeling okay today?" I asked.

"I'm okay. I'm feeling tired, and I've had a headache for several days," he replied.

"Why didn't you tell me until now?" I asked.

"Humpff." He grunted … like I was supposed to know what that meant.

If he really had been suffering from headaches all vacation, that would explain why he'd been so grumpy over the last couple of weeks. I couldn't understand why I had felt such uneasiness on our two-week holiday. Dean's reserved behavior and lack of excitement for halibut fishing three days before had me completely confused. But there was something else. I couldn't figure out the nagging feeling in the back of my neck.

I mentally accepted that checking out of our hotel early was for the best if we were both so ready to leave. So we packed our suitcases and left the hotel, forfeiting the prepayment on our very expensive room.

We were coming home from a two-week vacation from Vancouver to Tofino, ending in Victoria, BC, the day before. Traveling over Vancouver Island from Vancouver to the coast had been exhausting. I had done all the driving since Dean had not been himself. What little he had driven made me nervous, as he kept tailgating anyone he approached across the Vancouver Island pass, causing me to become very agitated. The scene from days before flashed again through my mind.

"Stop riding this guy's ass!" I nagged him yet again.

"Fine … fine …" he said.

No sooner would we pass a car than he would drive right up within a foot of the next car's bumper.

"DEAN!" I yelled. "You're doing it again!"

Uncharacteristically, he did not respond to my backseat driving but would pull away from the bumper of the vehicle in front of us. Not ten minutes later, he would do it again. After an hour of this, I insisted he pull over and let me drive.

Now, three days later, we were finally headed home. After we loaded the bikes and luggage from the room into the car, I headed out toward the ferry terminals to take us back to Washington.

I glanced at Dean from the driver's side of the car.

"Baby? Are you okay? You are awfully quiet."

"I'm okay." He looked at me a little alarmed. "Why do you keep asking me that?"

"I'm worried about you. You've had headaches for most of the trip, and you seem really zoned out. I want you to go to the doctor as soon as we get home," I told him.

"I just went to the doctor for a full checkup. Maybe it's the headaches making me tired. I've been taking Motrin regularly to try to get rid of them."

I thought about this information, worried that he was in pain.

"Do you have one right now?" I asked.

"Yeah, kinda dull, like it's lurking in the back of my brain."

I absorbed this information, filing it in the back of *my* brain while I maneuvered the car into the ticket line at the ferry terminal. We had a two-hour wait before leaving so we milled around the parking lot and walked to get an ice cream. During this time, I continue to watch him covertly. He was so withdrawn and abnormally quiet.

The ferry ride seemed to take hours before docking in Anacortes. There we disembarked and drove through customs, which took another hour. By then, it was dark out, and the air was humid with just enough bite that I needed to wear a sweater. As I drove the last couple of hours to get home, I could not help but notice that Dean stared straight ahead with a blank look on his face. I kept asking if anything was wrong—he was just so silent and didn't initiate conversation. He had become very withdrawn over the last few months, so it did not strike me as odd that he was so quiet, but I could not help noticing that he didn't sleep during the drive. Dean usually fell asleep when I drove home from date night or a late dinner, his mouth open in a snore. Internal silent alarms went off in my brain, but I didn't know what to make of his unusual behavior. We got home around midnight and went straight to bed, dumping our suitcases in the hall as we walked in the front door.

I awoke the next morning, invigorated to start my day; I had a lot of work to tackle from being on vacation. I was up early and left Dean to sleep in. I made his coffee and started cleaning up the suitcases we'd dropped hastily by the back door coming in late the night before. It was also my father's birthday, and I wanted to call to wish him happy birthday. Eventually, I decided to get a jump on my work for our business. As I worked on the computer with single-minded intensity, Dean finally woke up to have his morning coffee. Eventually, he walked by my office and asked, "What are you up to for the day?"

"I'm working." I said and told him of my plan to see my youngest daughter that day. "I'm going to head to Hannah's house and pick up the mail and accounting program to get the checking account updated for the business."

"I'm going to get busy too. I want to work in the yard and clean up the flower beds," he replied.

Another half hour went by and he meandered down the hall, again passing by my office. "What are you doing today?" he said.

Hmmm ... I thought to myself. *That is weird. Didn't he just ask me that?*

I replied absently again, "I'm working," still focused on reviewing the emails I needed to answer.

He then replied, "Sounds like my day too."

My subconscious was alerting me that it was strange he wasn't already outside. He never lingered in the morning, especially when he had a lot to do. Because my mind was distracted, I brushed the unsettled feelings aside and left the house to head to Buckley, where my daughter lived. Once there, I went over work issues with Hannah. But I couldn't shake the nagging feeling that I needed to get home. My daughter, her husband, Enrique, and my grandsons—Montego and Ruben—were headed to Buckley Days, the annual local fair, and I toyed with the idea of going with them, but I still had this subconscious urge to leave.

I said my goodbyes and decided not to stop at the grocery store on the way home to pick up fresh food for lunch. I really needed to get some meals in the house since we had been on vacation for two weeks, but I kept feeling more unsettled about going straight home.

No sooner had I pulled into the garage and gotten out of the car than Dean walked up to me from behind, coming from the open garage door. He was filthy. His shins, arms, and hands were covered in black mud, and his brow and neck were drenched in sweat. He was visibly upset.

"Hey, babe?" I said questioningly.

He immediately started to cry. Alarmed, I asked him what was wrong.

"I can't figure out how to get in the house."

I was confused but instantly reached out and hugged him, noticing his T-shirt was damp with perspiration. He began to sob on my shoulder, and I could tell it was from fear and emotional panic.

"It's okay," I said. "You're all right," I soothed as I spoke into his damp neck.

I immediately thought he must have had a heatstroke. He had been working in the garden all morning, and it was very hot and humid out. I led him to the back stoop and asked him to take off his shoes. He just looked at me crying, not knowing what I was asking. He did not know what to do. I helped him sit down and removed his muddy shoes. As I led him into the house, he kept rambling about how he couldn't figure out how to open the door.

"You must have a heatstroke. Let's get you cleaned up and cooled off, and I will try to figure things out."

I stripped him of his clothes and asked him to get in the shower. In addition to his confusion about untying his shoes, he could not figure out how to turn the water on. I quickly turned the shower knobs to the correct temperature, cleaned him up, and got him into bed. As he slowly calmed down, I asked him to rest, and I went into the office to research his symptoms. When I researched heat exhaustion online, it alarmed me that when it affects a person's mind, it is usually a sign of a stroke. Once I discovered that tidbit of information, I realized I had better call 911.

The fire department showed up quickly. They descended on the house like a SWAT team. Several men surrounded Dean in the bed, making the room look small. They looked foreign in our bedroom that was normally our private sanctuary, and I squirmed inside, wanting them to hurry and help Dean so they would leave.

As they ran tests, the EMT asked Dean what year it was.

He replied, "Uh, 1995?"

"Who is the president?"

Again, he replied incorrectly, "Bush?"

At this point, I was screaming in my head, *WHAT? Something is VERY wrong here.*

One of the firemen or EMTs suggested Dean may have had a stroke—or a TA, as he called it. They thought it was best to take him to the hospital.

Which one? I asked.

"How about Valley Medical?" he suggested.

I balked and said, "NO, I want him to go to Group Health in Bellevue."

I had heard bad things about Valley Medical, and even though it was closer, I didn't want their doctors examining Dean.

"His doctors are at Group Health. I want him to go there," I again demanded.

They argued a bit but finally agreed to go the extra distance. I left the room while they busily prepared to shift him from the bed to the stretcher and take him by ambulance to Overlake Hospital.

As I came outside on the porch, our neighbor Randy was standing there. He just looked at me and stepped forward to give me a hug. I completely lost it and started sobbing on his shoulder.

"I'm scared," I said. "Something is really wrong with him. I think he had a stroke."

I don't remember what he said in response. It didn't matter, as nothing would make me feel better. Somehow, I knew things were never going to be the same, and as I stepped off the front porch, the dread in my stomach intensified. I never did remember to call my dad and wish him a happy birthday.

DIAGNOSIS

In disbelief, I watched the EMTs load Dean into the ambulance and slowly pull out of our driveway. Like most summer days, the sun was out, and there was a beautiful blue sky above, in direct contrast to my dark, worried thoughts. Even after leaving our home in the country and driving into downtown Bellevue, I still managed to beat the ambulance to the hospital.

I had made the drive in forty-five minutes, and it was around 1:00 p.m. when I walked through the emergency room sliding doors in a panic, only to be told to stay in the waiting area until EMTs arrived. I could only sit with my stomach in knots and wonder if Dean was feeling scared that I was not with him. Once they arrived and admitted him, I met him in the assigned room. Dean was lying on the gurney they had set up in the sterile temporary cubicle. Next to us, I could hear people murmuring quiet words along with the beeping of medical equipment, and I felt sorry for them that they, too, had to be in a hospital on this beautiful summer day.

Suddenly, the doctor entered our room, sweeping the curtain aside with a flourish. "Hello, I'm the on-call doctor today, what seems to be the issue?" he said abruptly but with a slight smile on his face.

I explained Dean's symptoms and told him what had happened earlier at home.

He walked over to Dean and peered down at him, looking into his eyes and face.

"Hello, Dean, can I ask you some questions?" he said.

"Sure," Dean replied.

"What year is it?"

"Um, 1995?" Dean replied.

"What is your date of birth?"

"July 24, 1957?" Dean replied hesitantly, though it was the right answer.

"Who is our president?"

"Bush?"

The doctor shot me a slightly worried look. He did not comment on Dean's wrong answers; he only said, "We will get some blood work going right away, and I will schedule a CT scan so we can see what's going on. Do you have any questions?"

Dean and I both replied, "No."

As with most busy doctors, he turned around and swiftly left the room. A lab technician came in fairly quickly and took the blood samples.

While we waited for answers, I looked at Dean and asked him if he was doing okay. He nodded but closed his eyes; he looked exhausted and pale. I sat on a hard plastic chair next to him, for what seemed like forever, while we waited for the blood test results. I felt most tests should only take about thirty minutes, but when we were waiting in the emergency room, they seemed to take hours.

I had no patience, and I was tired from the long drive home from Victoria, BC, the day before. I wanted them to hurry up, so I could take Dean home, give him whatever medicine he needed, and make us some dinner. I really had no idea what was wrong with him or how seriously ill he was. I had no experience with anyone I loved ever being truly sick, so my mind did not allow me to grasp the severity of what was happening.

By now, Dean had calmed down, but I realized that he did not fully know what was happening. His behavior was almost childlike, and my motherly instincts were kicking in, wanting to protect him.

Finally, the technician came in and wheeled Dean out of the room to complete the CT scan. I waited anxiously in his room for his return. When I couldn't stand the waiting, I wandered into the hall, hoping for some relief. But I couldn't breathe, and my eyes welled up with tears that soon fell helplessly down my cheeks. I was embarrassed for anyone to see me lose control and quickly wiped my face with the back of my hand. It did help to release some of my emotions, and I was able to compose myself before the technician came back. I was somewhat sick to my stomach since I had not eaten anything for most of the day. The technician finally brought Dean back, and I continued to reassure him things would be okay.

Without warning, the doctor swept back into the room and said, "I'm sorry, but you have a mass in your brain. We do not know what it is, and we will have to send you to Virginia Mason, our downtown hospital, to have a neurosurgeon consult with you and review your scans. I will arrange for another ambulance to come and transport you to our Seattle facility."

He then awkwardly left the room without another word.

For several heartbeats, Dean and I sat in silence. I hesitantly looked at him, and he said, "Whoa! I did not see that coming!"

He then repeated the same phrase a couple more times.

I said nothing. I didn't know what to say. The silence itself was palpable. I was shell-shocked, not believing what I had heard. I did not comprehend or fully grasp how bad this diagnosis was. I was ashamed to admit—because I still did not understand the severity of his situation—, I immediately felt disappointed that we wouldn't be heading home, and that he was not going to get well quickly. It was a selfish thought, but it only lasted for a second. Luckily, neither one of us fully realized the months of hell in store for us. I looked at Dean in disbelief, and I was scared to read the emotions on his face. Finally, I leaned over him and looked directly into his eyes.

"Baby, whatever we are dealing with, we're going to beat it. You are the love of my life, and I will not lose you."

He smiled gratefully, and I could see that I had comforted him in a small way. By now it was close to 7:00 p.m. The new ambulance drivers, a man and a woman, showed up. They were very nice, joking with Dean to put him at ease. For the second time that day, I watched EMTs load Dean into an ambulance and drive away, lights flashing. My eyes filled with tears as I watched them take my love to yet another hospital. So much for my plans to get Dean home and resume a normal life. This was going to take much longer than I thought.

I wandered outside of the hospital and sat down in front of the entrance. I called my sister, Lisa. She is the one I always call in an emergency, because she is matter-of-fact and rational and always calms me down in tense situations.

"Please come get me," I said. "I'm freezing."

She said she would come right away and bring me a sweater. As

I sat on the curb in front of the hospital, waiting for my sister and brother-in-law to come pick me up and take me downtown, I tried to absorb everything that had just happened in the last four hours. I felt like a bomb had gone off in my brain and there was a big void where my normal thoughts were. I already missed Dean, and I had just left him with the ambulance crew. I could not fathom my life without him.

How did this happen? This was stuff that only happened to other people.

I was numb. Thinking too hard about what was going to happen was too painful, and beyond me at that point.

They finally arrived, and we headed to downtown Seattle to the Capital Hill area. I felt weird, sitting in the back seat of their car. I had not ridden with others, alone in the back of a car, in a long time.

Virginia Mason is a very old building in the heart of downtown. We quickly found an underground parking lot and trekked up the steep hill to find the entrance. Dean was on the thirteenth floor. The hospital rooms were small but private and had big windows to see the Seattle skyline. Dean was still very confused and didn't seem to know why he was there. I'm not sure he even remembered that he was told he had a brain tumor. I thought that was a good thing, as I didn't want to further upset him.

I only wished I could forget.

The surgeon, Dr. L, came in and basically told us he was going to run some similar tests that the emergency doctor had ran at Group Health, however, this time he was going to do an MRI. The MRI would give him much more detailed information about the mass, and where it was in the brain. They kept Dean overnight, running tests and stabilizing him with a steroid drug called Dexamethasone.

I left the hospital later that night, around 10:00 p.m. I felt so dejected to be going home without him. Luckily, they stabilized him with a drug, and I was able to take him home the next day. But there was no drug that could treat the terror I felt at the uncertainty of what was to become of us.

CRANIOTOMY DAY

Dean's surgeon wanted to schedule his biopsy surgery in the first available time slot, which was three days after his diagnosis. So we drove downtown to Virginia Mason hospital once again for his craniotomy. It was another bright sunny day in Seattle, and it seemed surreal that the world continued to revolve as normal, when my life as I knew it was forever changed. I was terrified of losing Dean to brain cancer. His imminent death lurked like a black aura behind me, but I refused to acknowledge its existence.

How will I go on living without him?

What will happen to our business? Can I afford to stay in our home?

What if he dies today during surgery?

Questions popped in and out of my head like puffs of smoke, making me wonder what I would do if he were gone. I stuffed the thoughts deep down inside and did not examine them too closely. I could not come to terms with his death, so I refused to think he really would die.

Dean was feeling very nervous and weak from lack of food, as he was not allowed to eat the morning of a surgery. Unfortunately, his surgery was not scheduled first for the day. I had started my day at the early hour of 5:00 a.m. to get to the hospital on time.

Our instructions showed that the surgeon needed an MRI using special nodes stuck to Dean's head so that Dr. L could map out where he was going to drill into Dean's brain. Group Health contracted with Virginia Mason hospital, and due to poor protocol communication, our MRI tech was delayed. I was already upset and worried, and this setback only caused me further anxiety that things would not go well. My stepdaughter, Karly, showed up for support, and it was nice to have her wait with me, since I felt so alone with the weight of every decision on my shoulders. I went up to the front desk again to ask the receptionist to find our tech, as I did not want to miss our surgery time. I approached the desk nervously, and she smiled to reassure me as I walked closer.

"I will notify you just as soon as I locate your tech," she said. She was very accommodating and apologized for the delay.

"Thank you so much. My husband is very anxious, and I just want everything to go well," I replied before walking back to my seat.

Already, my battle to look out for my husband was beginning. Every phase of his treatment required me to question, fight, and decide on how to move forward. The tech finally showed up, complaining that he had been unable to find the "nodes" he needed and gone back to another part of the hospital to get them. "Hurry up and wait" became the motto of this illness and all treatment associated with it.

Finally, Dean's MRI was complete, and he was ready to go on to the next phase. The three of us arrived at the surgery hall, and I was relieved that we were on time.

Quickly, I strode up to the front desk to check Dean in. The receptionist calmly apologized, "I'm so sorry, the patient currently in surgery has gone beyond the expected time, so Dean's surgery will be delayed."

I could tell that this happened all the time and that there was nothing to be done about it. I sat down next to Dean to let him know what the delay was. He was already feeling poorly due to lack of food and water, and I felt horrible that he had to wait longer than necessary. My nerves were giving me an upset stomach, and I could only imagine how scared he was, combined with feeling weak from not being able to eat or drink. The room was full of people who were anxiously biding time just like we were, trying to find ways to keep busy while they nervously milled around, chatting to others around them. The waiting area was hot and smelled like nervous sweat, mixed with differing perfumes and deodorant. I felt suffocated.

Sitting and waiting was intolerable. I kept thinking of them drilling Dean's skull open and touching his brain. It was terrifying for me to ponder this—I couldn't imagine what Dean felt.

Around 2:00 p.m. (two hours past his scheduled time) the nurses finally called him back. I felt relieved that he would no longer be uncomfortable from the delay. They still had to prep him, though, and surgery was to take two hours; afterward, he would go straight to post-op. By this time, Karly's boyfriend, Matt, had stopped by to help out. He decided to stay in the waiting area in case Dean's number was called so Karly and I could go and get some food. While we were gone, Matt called to notify us that Dean was out of surgery. I was surprised at how quickly this procedure went, and we ran anxiously back. Even though the surgery took less than two hours, there were so many similar operations being performed simultaneously that there was not an available bed to put him in. He sat in post-op recovery for over three hours. During this time, a nurse called us back to a small room, where there was a table and three chairs. Still wearing his green scrubs, Dr. L briskly walked into the room.

He smiled and said, "Everything went as planned. Now we wait."

"What does that mean?" I asked, bewildered.

"Well, we won't know if the brain suffered any damage during the procedure until he wakes up."

"Do you know what it is yet?"

"I don't know what the biopsy will reveal. However, the brain matter was gray, and that is not the normal color."

I was frustrated, scared, and confused. I both wanted and didn't want to know what the mass was. What if it was a glioma, the worst kind of brain cancer? I wanted to fix everything, and I felt if I knew what I was dealing with, I could find the answer and make this problem go away.

I thanked Dr. L, and he left the room.

The nurse took pity on me after Dean had been a couple hours in post-op. She knew I was frustrated and worried, wanting to see him and be with him so I could reassure myself he was okay. She called me back and said I could visit him in the temporary area where they put surgery patients until they find them a room. Dean's head was heavily bandaged, and he was not coherent. He did acknowledge Karly and me, and I was so relieved that he knew me and seemed fine. I was only able to stay a few minutes because I wasn't supposed to be back in that area.

I was exhausted when they finally called me to let me know they had found Dean a room. I ran to the designated floor and room number only to find he still wasn't there yet. My frustration from delay after delay was palpable. I could barely restrain my anger and impatience; all that combined with my lack of sleep made me feel like a ticking time bomb. I contained my relief when he was wheeled into the room. I was finally able to sit with him a couple of hours and make sure he was okay before giving myself permission to go home after 11:00 p.m. for much-needed sleep. The next day, when family came to visit, I couldn't help myself and climbed into bed with him. I desperately craved his touch already. I needed reassurance that he would be okay. He just curved his arm behind my neck and held me close as I curled into his side. He smiled, and I immediately felt comforted.

Surprisingly, for someone who'd just had his skull cracked open, Dean recovered quickly. Within the next twenty-four hours, I was able to check him out to go home. It was wonderful that it only took him about a week to feel better, but he was still on the Dexamethasone drug, a nasty steroid. I was anxious for him to continue taking it because, after his initial diagnosis, he regained his ability to think. To me, that drug made Dean act and think normally, so I could pretend he was going to be fine. I did not realize that it was like trading his soul with the devil. It served one purpose—to reduce swelling and pain—but left on it for any length of time, he suffered very detrimental side effects. Since I hadn't seen the damage it could do, I didn't realize how bad it would be.

I missed Dean terribly. True, I was with him constantly, but I'm not talking about his physical self. My confidant, my rock was nowhere to be found. The man I spoke with every day about my fears and troubles was gone. I hated that I could not talk to him about him! I was protecting him already, like my child. I could not upset him with my fears and questions. Even when he was recuperating in the hospital bed, I was desperate to feel his masculinity and breathe in his smell. I wanted him to continue to be my pillar of strength, but unfortunately, he was now and forever different. We were switching roles, and I hated it.

ALCOHOL AND GBM

During the next month while we waited for Dean's prognosis, we lived in a state of hope and anxiety. Dean's step dad, Jim, and his girlfriend, Cherie, showed up unannounced for a visit once he heard the news, but Dean was not ready to face anyone. His mind was still processing the possibility of death, and he was in a fog of fear, unable to talk about the mass in his brain. I believed it was too painful for him, not to mention that he wasn't fully in his right mind anymore. All the idiosyncrasies of his behavior in the last year were finally revealed to me in a different light. The mood swings, unhappiness, forgetfulness, and remoteness—it all made sense. In a way, I was grateful that he hadn't become unhappy with me or our marriage, but of course, I was unhappy to learn that a brain tumor was responsible for the changes.

When these visitors first arrived at our home, it felt like an obligation to host them, but in reality, after they stayed a while, it was good to see them. Jim loved Dean so much and just wanted to see if he was okay. I could tell Dean wasn't able to engage emotionally, and he showed a façade that everything was going to be okay when interacting with both Jim and Cherie. But when he was alone with me, his demeanor reflected the stress of being forcibly social.

Since I didn't know they were coming, I'd made plans beforehand to run errands, which meant I left Dean to entertain them while I was gone.

When I returned, I found them all congregated in the living room, talking.

"Hi, baby," I said.

"How was your day?"

"We had a nice time. We went to the store and picked up some groceries to make a nice dinner," he said happily.

I was relieved that he seemed to be acting relaxed and gregarious.

"We're going to barbecue some meat and have corn on the cobb with salad. Does that sound good?"

"Absolutely! Works for me!" I said as I walked into the bedroom to change my clothes.

It was a beautiful sunny day, and we decided to cook and eat outside in the backyard by the waterfall. My brother Tony walked into the backyard.

"Grab a plate, Tony, and have some dinner with us," I said. "Have you met Dean's stepdad and his wife?"

"It's really nice to meet you." Tony shook Jim's hand and nodded at Cherie.

We all sat down to eat dinner, and around this time I noticed Dean was very quiet.

"How are you doing, babe?" I asked him.

"I'm good," he quickly replied.

I decided to leave him alone and went back to making conversation with everyone until it was time to clean up the dinner dishes.

Jim and Cherie left soon after dinner, as they could see Dean was tired and his energy was fading fast. We walked them to the door to wave them off, but as we turned to go back into the house, I noticed Dean stumbled a bit and was walking unevenly.

Immediately, I worried that something was going on in his head with the tumor.

"Oh my God, baby, are you feeling okay?" I asked. "You aren't walking straight."

"I'm FINE," he insisted. "Theerresh nushing wrong wish me," he slurred.

"Have you been drinking?" I demanded.

"No!" he emphatically denied.

I peered up into his face and looked closely into his eyes. I doubted his word. He had lied to me in the past about drinking, so I had good reason to question his answer now.

"Oh my God, Dean! You are slurring your words, and you aren't walking right. I need to take you to the ER!"

"NO! I'm FINE!" he yelled. "I'm NOT GOINGSH!"

I ignored his anger and rushed out of the room to find my car keys. I was worried sick that he was having a seizure or the tumor was growing. I didn't know what was happening and needed to get him to a hospital. I last left Dean in the living room, but then heard him in the bathroom. Suddenly, I heard a crash and thump, so I went running through the living room screaming his name.

"Dean. Dean! Are you okay?" I cried out.

Dean had been sitting on the toilet and had fallen off onto the floor. He was embarrassed and flustered, huffing in silent outrage. Tony and I ran to him, but he shook us off as we reached out to help him up.

"Dean, get in the car. We are going to the hospital! Please hurry!" I yelled at him.

He followed me, protesting the entire way out to the car.

I backed up out of the driveway in a big hurry. It was 9:00 p.m. by then and getting dark.

The hospital was an hour from our house, but since it was after hours, I took the main freeway, hoping for no traffic. Dean was silent for quite a while but then started to yell at me that he wanted to go home.

"Baby, I'm just going to have you checked out to make sure everything is okay. You shouldn't be slurring or falling over. Something is wrong."

"This is fucking bullshit!" he said. "I want to go home."

I was shocked at his anger and a little taken aback that he was so adamant. Right then, Hannah called me in a panic. She wanted me to call 911, as she couldn't find her husband, Enrique, and she was in horrible pain.

"Mom, it hurts sooo bad. I need help," she cried into the phone.

Suddenly, Dean tried to grab the steering wheel of the car while I was driving sixty miles an hour on the freeway. He was trying to turn the car around on a three-lane freeway when the opposite direction was on the other side of a concrete barrier.

"Oh my God! What are you doing?" I screamed.

Hannah was still on the phone. "Mom, it feels like I'm dying. What do I do?"

"HANG UP the phone and call 911," I screamed. "I'm so sorry, I can't help you right now. I'm rushing Dean to the ER, and he is fighting me. I have to go. Call me back as soon as you can!"

I started to cry. Dean was not acting like the man I knew he was, and I recognized that the tumor was changing him quickly. I felt so alone and scared, and I was worried about Hannah. It made me sick that I could not be there to help her.

I drove as fast as I could to get to Bellevue. I begged Dean to please calm down. Everything would be okay once we saw the doctor. Finally, I made it to the hospital without crashing and rushed Dean into the ER waiting area to check him in. I explained he was having speech issues and his balance was off. I was worried it was the brain tumor.

They rushed him into a small office where the nurse took his vitals and asked what was happening. While I explained his behavior and what I observed to be unusual for his speech and balance, he became more and more belligerent. He would interrupt me and tell me he wanted to leave. When they checked him into a room, I quietly begged him to please be patient. I just wanted the doctor to make sure he was okay.

The lab tech showed up to take his blood, and the doctor came in and let us know he was ordering a CT scan to see if there were changes in the mass in his brain. Dean was openly angry and irritated but followed orders. Finally, the CT Tech came to take him to imaging.

I continued to pace, and I finally got a chance to call Hannah. She had called 911, and the ambulance came to pick her up. Enrique stayed back at home with their two young sons. Hannah was having a gallbladder attack and needed to have it removed. Guilt washed over me that I was not there to be by her side.

The stress was overwhelming, and I suddenly, felt like I was going to collapse. I wandered out into the hall to have a good cry, much like I did the first time we were there for Dean's initial diagnosis. As I hid behind a door by the nurse's station, I worked to gather my composure. The nurse that was assigned to Dean saw me. "I have the blood work back. He's drunk!" she said in a disgusted way.

"Are you fucking kidding me?" I could not hide my outrage.

Then, Dean came running down the hallway. The CT technician was chasing him with the gurney and begging him to please lie back down.

Dean ran into his room, the back of his gown flapping behind him, showing his bare butt. If I hadn't been in shock at his behavior, I would have laughed out loud. It just felt like my life continued to spiral out of control in such ridiculous ways. The numbness of my situation was wearing off, and I was horrified by how far things with Dean had progressed in such a short time. And I was angry that, not only was I dealing with his cancer, but now his behavior changes too.

"What is going on?" I demanded, alarmed.

"He jumped off the table and took off running. I barely got the CT scan done," the technician barked. He shook his head in disgust and walked back to his wing as I ran into the room after Dean.

"You are drunk!" I screamed at him. "How could you do this to me? I ASKED you if you had any alcohol, and you denied it emphatically. WHY would you make us go through this when it would have been easier to tell me the truth?"

"I only had one beer—it was nothing."

"When did you get the beer? Why wouldn't you just tell me? You put me through HELL tonight. Do you realize my daughter is very sick and I could not be there to help her? This is absolutely the WORST thing you have ever done to me," I snapped.

"I'm leaving!" is all he said. He gathered his clothes, put them on, and started walking down the hallway toward the exit.

The nurse came running up. "Hey, we need to check you out before you can leave," she said.

"Good luck stopping him. I can't hold him back." I was so angry I didn't care what he did at that point.

I ran down the hall to catch up with him and told him to wait at the curb so I could go get the car.

When I drove up from the parking garage, the nurse was outside standing next to Dean and had brought him the discharge papers to sign. I pulled up to the entrance and told him to get in.

He started to speak, but I cut him off, "Don't say a word. I'm am the maddest I have ever been at you right now. What you did was horrible, and I need to calm down."

He shut up, and we drove in silence the entire way home. My heart was full of anguish. I knew this wasn't the real Dean, but I had to deal with who he was now. Luckily, Hannah got into surgery and had a successful procedure the next day, and I was able to go and be with her.

After I thought long and hard about Dean's behavior, I realized something. The subdued change in his happiness had been slowly coming on for a year. The subtleties of his personality, like his sense of humor, caring nature, and outgoing friendliness were muted somehow. Only I had noticed the changes in his persona. It was like all the joy he had once carried around with him, was gone. Something inside him knew that he couldn't feel happiness. He knew all was not quite right, but he could not figure out what it was. In an effort to *feel* normal, he turned to alcohol to be happier. I wondered if the tumor stopped his brain's ability to produce serotonin in his body and he was looking for anything to replace it. I truly believed that somehow this was the answer to his behavior, so I forgave him. But not for a day or two.

The next day, I showed no compassion for his hangover. I also found out that alcohol affects someone with a brain tumor much stronger than a healthy person. I made him get up early to have breakfast and say goodbye to his stepdad. He was somber and quiet, and later he apologized for his behavior. Ultimately, I could not stay mad or blame him for long. He was living in hell, and I couldn't predict how I would handle myself under the same circumstances. We would just have to get through whatever was thrown at us. Hopefully, we would survive it.

PATHOLOGY

If anyone had told me that I would be spending my summer waiting on pathology to tell me what was growing in my husband's brain, I would never have believed them. I could only hope that it was all a huge mistake, or that it was just a benign growth or cyst that would be easily removable.

After Dean's biopsy, Dr. L told me that it could be either of those things; worst-case scenario, it could be multiple sclerosis or a glioma. He would not speculate even a little because he said he had been wrong in the past and did not want to give me false information. I was hoping for MS over a glioma but still didn't truly know what that disease entailed either.

Dean and I waited for over three weeks to get the diagnosis, even though we were told it should only take three days. During that time, I prayed, hoped for the best, and tried to distract myself with the daily minutia of life. I was still numb and in shock at that point, and I was scared to feel beyond what I knew, so I tried to remain positive for Dean's sake. My emotions were on a roller coaster, and inside I was freaking out and planning my next move for when we finally had answers. My continued research on the Internet for anything regarding brain tumors was terrifying. I blocked the worst information, telling myself that what I found didn't apply to Dean; his case was different.

During this time, Dean and I bonded emotionally, preparing to do battle as a team. Dean was still in denial for the most part and would alternate between fear, despair, and a "we're going to beat this" attitude. Deep down, my intuition was telling me that the results were going to be bad, but when facing the incomprehensible, I tried to argue myself into a false state of calm.

As the weeks passed and we waited on the pathology results, I started making calls, hounding the doctors to move forward with a plan. I felt precious time slipping away. I was in a panic but kept my concerns from Dean because I wanted to protect him as much as possible. I went ahead and scheduled appointments with the radiologist and oncologist so that when we finally had some answers, we would not have to waste more time waiting on the doctors' availability. Another lesson I learned through this process is that specialist doctors are booked out two to three months. It's insane how hard it is to get an appointment when faced with a life-threatening illness. I felt like yelling, "Hello? What is wrong with our medical system? Where are all the doctors?"

It seemed every time a new building went up in our neighborhood, it was a medical building of some sort. Yet every doctor Dean needed to see was unavailable for weeks, sometimes months. Dealing with scheduling appointments alone incited my anger and frustration throughout this process. Wasn't caring for my sick husband enough to deal with?

While coping with all the medical and physical changes in my husband, I learned to live in the present. If one doctor or treatment plan was unavailable to me, then I moved on to another. I never stopped looking, researching, or hoping to find an answer to what his diagnosis could mean.

Soon enough, and after many frustrating calls to the surgeon's office and nursing team, Dr. L finally called that fateful July day. He talked with Dean first, and I could tell that it was not good news. Dean's face took on a look of resignation and fear, as he huddled over his cell phone. He paced outside in the front yard as he listened to what the doctor was telling him. My eyes followed him as he moved restlessly from the yard to the front porch, and I felt the pain he was experiencing as if it were my own. I could tell the conversation was winding down, and I asked Dean to hand me the phone so I could speak directly with Dr. L. I wasted no time, fired off my questions like bullets.

"What is it?"

"What's our next step?"

"How reliable are the test results?"

"Why can't we resect the tumor?"

His answers were plain and direct, "Well, it's a glioma about five centimeters in diameter, Stage 3 or 4."

"The sample was small, and pathology had a hard time diagnosing the exact stage of the cancer, so they sent it to Washington State University for a second opinion. Regardless, Stage 3 or 4 is treated the same, so we suggest you move forward with the protocol treatment as soon as possible."

"As we discussed during the craniotomy, we are unable to resect his tumor due to the location."

I could hear him telling me the information, but the shock didn't allow me to process what this fully meant. All I could comprehend was that he did not say glioblastoma (which is the deadliest of all brain cancer), therefore it wasn't the worst possible news. I did not understand that a Stage 4 glioma is the same as glioblastoma and that either one was a death sentence. My mind worked fast to process the information he was giving me. I was trying to figure out what my next steps were for Dean's survival, all while thinking—*How is this fucking happening? How am I going to fix this? There must be a way out of this hell that has become our life.*

At this point, losing my husband was not an option. The call ended quickly once I realized asking further questions was not going to change the diagnosis.

To feel useful with a modicum of control over the awful situation, I continued to be proactive with scheduling the next doctor appointments, researching the disease, and handling all the medications. Once this illness arrived, my entire life became about the next medical test, treatment, and doctor visit. There were regular MRIs, blood work, radiation mask fittings, and scheduled medications. There were so many pills, all being taken at differing intervals. On top of that, we added holistic medical care to the treatment plan that had Dean hooked up to IVs four hours a day. I didn't have time to think about long-term results, as I was so busy dealing with every minute of every day cooking, cleaning, driving to appointments, dispensing medicine, and running our company.

When Dean finally went in to have the second MRI to prep for radiation and chemotherapy, it had already been a long day. Afterward,

I tucked the manila folder with the latest MRI results into my purse to sit down and peruse later after we got home and had dinner. I didn't think too much about the report, as I was busy performing my everyday mundane tasks of dealing with work and cooking a healthy ketogenic dinner for Dean. I completed all my chores and made my way into the office for a quick peek at the test results, before sitting down next to my husband to watch a little TV and de-stress from the day.

Unfortunately, as I started to read the report, I realized that in the span of three weeks that nasty tumor had already grown almost an entire centimeter. As I read the radiologist's report, saw the tumor measurements comparing the diagnosed date tumor size to the current tumor size, my body went cold and my stomach dropped, like I was on a ride at Six Flags. I stood up, and my mind felt like it was floating next to my body. Inside, I was silently screaming in horror at this knowledge. I stumbled out of the office and started crying. Dean walked down the hall toward me, and I went into the beginnings of an anxiety attack. I couldn't breathe, and I was mumbling and crying hysterically. Dean couldn't figure out what was going on. I didn't want to upset him, but I felt like I was going to explode.

"The tumor has grown," I finally gasped. "We have to DO something now."

It was too late to call the radiologist or oncologist, as they were closed for the day. I would have to suffer through the night until I could go back into battle and start calling doctors in the morning to get things into action. Dean tried to comfort me, and helped me calm down. He held me and stroked my hair, and I felt some comfort from his arms, but in the back of my mind I was realizing he was going to die soon and I couldn't stop it.

RADIATION AND CHEMO

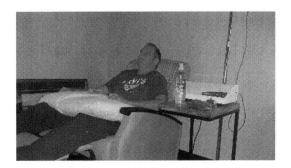

Dean used to tell me he had nightmares of the long hallway that led from the underground parking lot to the radiology department at Group Health on Capitol Hill.

For forty-six days, I gently woke Dean up at 5:30 a.m. and helped him get dressed and loaded into the car. By 6:00 a.m. I was fighting traffic over the Highway 18 pass that connected to the I-90 freeway that led me to downtown Seattle by 8:00 a.m. On a good day, I could make the drive in ninety minutes, but it would usually take us over two hours one way. Just the drive alone caused a lot of daily stress for me. I had to incorporate the tedious travel into our routine, in addition to all the other doctors' appointments and scheduled medications.

Early into treatment, Dean was physically able to get out of the car and walk through the automated sliding doors that led into a lower atrium of the hospital. He suffered from some fatigue but was still walking every day and moving around like normal. Unfortunately, after only a couple of weeks, due to the radiation and chemo, he was unable to find their office without help. By the end of treatment, he would hobble with a cane like an eighty-year-old man, and I would need to assist him everywhere he went, as he had mentally lost his ability to function.

Every day of radiation, I would help him to walk down this long hallway, a dull color of yellow and green that reminded me of diarrhea, to get to the waiting room for his next dose. Dean, like so many others having radiation, had his head immobilized by a mask that was screwed to the table. The mask looked like Jason from the Halloween horror movie, only straps of plastic instead of eyeholes. When he was fitted for the contraption, he expressed to me his angst and dismay at that part of the procedure. It was frightening, and I felt that he was so brave to endure this. Quickly, he lost the power to complete tasks, remember short-term daily events, and figure out time and dates. But worst of all, he lost his ability to enjoy life. He would come home and sit outside for hours, doing nothing—just staring blankly ahead. I kept thinking of how he had always been so active, never able to sit still.

What was he thinking? I often wondered to myself.

Maybe he needed to decompress, meditate, or reflect. But the habit of sitting and staring at nothing for hours never went away. The daydreaming only got worse, and I secretly hated that I had lost the essence of him. He was no longer checked into life; therefore, he had checked out of mine. I likened it to the doctors giving him a lobotomy. It was such a radical change from his old personality and a constant reminder that he was no longer the same man I had married.

During this time, I was hyperfocused on saving Dean's life, and I was in denial of his prognosis. I spent hours researching on the Internet, reading books, and going to websites, like The American Brain Cancer website, and Cancer Compass. I still did not understand why doctors could not cut the tumor out or kill it in place. I found a procedure called NeuroBlate—a process in which they laser the tumor and heat it up, cooking the tissue to kill it from within and not affect the surrounding tissue—that I wanted a surgeon to try on Dean. I tried calling the doctors in Cleveland and San Diego that did this procedure. I learned that it's very costly to get medical care in another state. Medical insurance does not travel state to state. For a procedure such as this, it could cost in excess of $250,000. I tried many times to call the San Diego facility to reach the surgeon who was trained on this procedure and never got a return call.

In the meantime, we added full holistic care to Dean's treatment plan. After his radiation and chemo, I would drive him to Bellevue, where he would have IVs of BOT—a procedure where a liter of blood is withdrawn, sterilized, and infused with oxygen, then dripped through an IV back into the body—Artesunate, or hydrogen peroxide. These IVs would run up to four hours at a time and four to five days a week. Our lives quickly became nonstop medical treatments. They consumed hours of every day. I looked forward to the weekends, as it felt like I had a forty-hour-a-week job, driving to all the appointments then trying to work on the side at the same time, only on the go. Dean was on ten to fifteen supplements at a time. Some of them were disgusting to swallow, and he struggled with it at first; eventually, he fought me on taking them altogether. It was exhausting to keep track of what he took daily and at what time. Dean had no way to do this for himself. He soon got tired of all the treatments and began resisting all of the holistic procedures.

At first, I had the hardest time accepting that Dean did not show initiative to research or investigate his own illness. He never asked questions, made suggestions, or showed any interest in different procedures. I was so driven to fix everything that I thought I was enough for the both of us. I kept up this pace for several months. It helped me feel like I had control and that I was doing something or that I could change the prognosis. After all, there were other long-term survivors. I read a book called *Radical Remissions* over and over; it was a book that brought me hope. There were many stories of people who healed themselves from the brink of death by changing their lives and forgoing Western medicine. Mostly, the stories recounted how standard treatments in our country had failed them and they were out of options, so they turned to alternative methods of survival. I had a niggling doubt while I read this book that these were people healing *themselves*; it was not a loved one doing it for them. I would try to convince Dean to find this personal nirvana that would heal him. I wanted him to "get it."

This meant he needed to find a spiritual peace, a peace I knew he did not have—peace with God, peace with dying, or peace with his life. I could not convince him that he needed to apply this mental focus to getting better. And after many frustrating conversations, I would end up crying in anguish. I wept because I knew deep down that he *could not* understand, not that he *would not* understand. Only over time did I fully realize that Dean never had the mental ability to diagnose himself, research medical information, or be proactive about his care. He had the tumor long before we knew of its existence, and it was so large when it was finally discovered that it had subtly taken away more faculties than I wanted to admit. Combined with the radiation, Dean's mental ability to function on a normal level was completely and irreversibly gone.

LIVING WITH GBM

Dean and I pushed forward into treatment with a modicum of hope and resolution. Unfortunately, we made his treatment decisions based on fear. Looking back, I would have done things differently. In addition, we were aggressive in attacking the tumor using all different methods so we would have no regrets, but that was not necessarily the best plan. I mentioned that in addition to chemo and radiation we included holistic treatments. Treatment included varying IVs called B.O.T (Bio Oxidated Therapy/Ozone therapy), Vitamin C, and Artesunate, ending with CoQ10 injections. Based on other patients using this plan, I believe that the B.O.T. are highly effective and have had very positive results on patients with tumors that have been resected.

As soon as Dean was diagnosed, I researched everything I could find on Glioblastoma. One of the books I read was from Ben Williams. Ben Williams is somewhat of an icon or hero in the GBM world. Around twenty years ago, he was a professor and was diagnosed with GBM. He went through the protocol chemo and radiation but decided to research alternative methods, taking a different approach to the deadly outcome of standard treatment. He researched previous clinical trials and their outcomes and noted that certain drugs and or supplements had adverse effects on GBM. For various reasons, the trials had been scrapped by the hosting Pharma companies. Ben then took a "cocktail" of these individual supplements and drugs for nonrecurrence of his tumor. He talked of having to drive to Mexico to get these drugs over the counter, as his oncologist in the States would not prescribe them.

I feel there is a real problem in this country in treating this disease, and only the public can demand reform. Ultimately, it costs Pharma companies up to $400 million to get a drug through FDA approval. That doesn't account for the cost to get the Pharma companies to even consider it, let alone do Phase I-IV clinical trials. Since there are an estimated thirty thousand brain tumors diagnosed per year, the money does not pencil out. Pharma companies are not going to invest in a drug that won't recoup a profit.

My experience of the current Western Medicine's plan to treat GBM played out in confusion, frustration, and then anger. Once surgery is no longer necessary with GBM, the surgeon is finished with a patient's care. Other than consulting with other doctors when necessary, he does not interact further with the patient. The next step was to consult with an oncologist and radiologist. Their role is to determine dosage of chemo and strength of radiation, from what seemed to be based mostly on weight—maybe height, age, and location of tumor as well. They referred to a calculation of sorts but always seemed to ask us for Dean's weight as a determining factor.

They then put the patient on a regimen of daily chemo and radiation at five days a week for six weeks. Once the radiation is complete, then the radiologist steps out of the picture, and the patient is left with the oncologist. The oncologist cares for the patient until he or she is no longer needed and/or the patient dies.

I have always understood that a doctor is a person who assesses an individual's health to determine an illness then treats that person to cure him or her. In the world of GBM, there is no cure. If someone does happen to live longer than predicted, it's an anomaly. Every brain cancer patient that comes in is given the same protocol treatment with the same predicted lifespan, so the job of a radiologist and oncologist is just to prolong the lifespan with no real long-term outcome. With standard lifespan being six to eighteen months.

There is no doubt that Dean would have been dead in less than two months if we had done nothing, mostly because his tumor was so large when first found and was unresectable. However, the true and detailed consequences of radiation and chemo were not told to me by the doctors. I was never told that radiation weakens the blood vessels in GBM patients, which are already naturally weakened by the tumor. I was never told that chemo commonly causes blood clots in conjunction with cancer and that treatment would involve blood thinners that work adversely with vessels that have been radiated on. All I seem to remember was getting some literature handed to me explaining side effects, mostly vomiting and tiredness.

When learning that Dean had an inoperable brain tumor, I did what the doctors suggested and followed protocol without a true understanding of the big picture. Fear pushed me along in the journey, and to delve too deeply into my emotions and question what was happening was unbearable because then I would have to "feel" that my worst nightmare had come true. Ignorance was bliss at that time, but I couldn't stay that way for long. I ran out of options.

Consider this list I made of the realities I learned through experience but was never told by the radiologist or oncologist:

1. Glioblastomas weaken the veins in your brain and are prone to "bleeding."

2. Radiation can help or precipitate the bleeding in the brain.

3. Chemo with cancer causes blood clots in a substantial percentage of recipients.

4. Blood clots cause pulmonary embolism—a deadly side effect.

5. The main FDA-approved chemotherapy drug is Temozolomide. This drug was approved in 1999 and breaks the blood-brain barrier. Unfortunately, it works better with tumors that are methylated, and most doctors do not even test the tissue to see if it's methylated or non-methylated. Most tumors are non-methylated.

6. Dexamethasone causes loss of vision and other severe side effects.

This information is all tied together in a sick treatment plan that ultimately does not work to save lives but hopes to extend life by maybe a year at best.

There came a point during Dean's treatment when I'd uncovered these truths and it all became too much. Out of frustration one morning, I navigated to the ABTA website and posted the following excerpt. I am sharing it now in hopes of helping others who are in a similar situation. The response at the time I posted it was all positive and encouraging. Being involved on the site gave me an invisible comfort, feeling I was included in this club for desperate individuals trying to survive, care for those who might die, or had lost a loved one.

I woke up at 4:00 a.m. one morning and couldn't sleep yet another night, all the thoughts running through my head of what my life had become, I made a list of all the things I had learned from my husband's brain tumor for any of those out there who have just been diagnosed and are looking for information.

1. *Don't decide your treatment plan out of fear.*

2. *No two people respond the same with this disease.*

3. *Don't let doctors scare you with their statistics and warnings of imminent death. WE had our bad experience with a neurosurgeon that was a huge jerk. They are not GOD. They cannot predict when you are going to die. If a surgeon can't operate, he has no interest in your well-being. Once the radiologist is done, he is finished with you as well. Your only source of help beyond the protocol treatment is the oncologist if you are not seeing a naturopathic doctor.*

4. *CAREFULLY decide if you want to do radiation or chemo or both (There ARE other options).*

5. *Research clinical trials prior to all treatments. Some won't take new patients, depending on prior treatments received. Clinical-trials.org is a good source.*

6. *Chemo causes blood clots, which can give you pulmonary embolisms.*

7. *Radiation can cause your brain to bleed, be careful if you get clots and then proceed to use blood thinners.*

8. *Dexamethasone causes muscle atrophy and will severely decrease*

the muscles in your pelvic, quads, and shoulder areas. Try to keep this drug to a minimum. It is really hard to get off this drug as well. Your own body's adrenals stop producing when this steroid takes over, and when you withdraw it causes depression, lack of appetite, and mental/physical deficits that are unique to each person. In addition, it reduces your vision.

9. *Radiation can kill your good brain cells as well as bad. You may never be the same mentally.*

10. *This cancer becomes your life. (It becomes the caregiver's life as well). Doctor appointments, dispensing medication, physical therapy, counseling, and in my case, full help with dressing, eating, and going places).*

11. *Diet changes DO help.*

12. *Find a naturopath or holistic doctor to complement your treatment plan, OR use their treatment plan. They can create a cocktail of drugs to help you fight this without chemo to poison the body.*

13. *Your body can develop the tumor for differing reasons, but whatever the reasons are, your body was weakened, and the cancer cells took over where your good cells could not fight it off. You must support your immune system to naturally fight it off. This is your best defense.*

14. *Your balance may be affected as was my husband's and you fall. These falls can cause other complications, which then become painful situations to deal with on a daily basis. Find good support for that person to get around, or make a safe environment for them to get to the bathroom during the night.*

15. *Rick Simpson GOLD Cannabis paste is amazing and can bring a personality back to life, help with pain, and help fight the cancer*

cells. You should try to break the brain barrier with this and insert it rectally for the best results; however, my husband could not tolerate that, so we put it under his tongue.

16. *Your loved one will most likely no longer be a source of strength to share in the daily struggles of work, chores, and life. You will become the caregiver and lose the support role of your spouse. The dynamic of your relationship changes forever. This is where I suffer grief eventually.*

17. *As the caregiver, I suffered from these emotions in somewhat order: Fear, sadness, determination, hope, acceptance, anger, guilt, and grief. There is love and happiness in there, too, but these were the main emotions as stuff happened.*

18. *I found that a housekeeper and organic paleo food delivery service have been invaluable.*

19. *Depending on the diagnosed person, not all patients are CAPABLE of having a great attitude, willingness to fight, and taking treatment graciously. So for those caregivers out there who are dealing with a sick loved one they are trying to help live, don't feel bad that you are doing all the fighting. They are probably just not capable of it themselves, and it is one more challenge God has given us to fight. You are not alone.*

20. *Lastly, always see a neuroSPECIALIST for brain surgery, treatment, and advice. And get the tissue to a pathology treatment place so you can fight your tumor with the drugs that it is least resistant to. Why take a chemo that won't even work?*

During Dean's illness, I stopped sleeping. I would wander upstairs most every night to think, watch TV, or get on the computer to do more research. As time went quickly, I watched Dean continue to lose cognitive and physical abilities, which was crushing. I was still in denial that Dean would die, believing I could save his life. But when symptoms were undeniable, I had to acknowledge that his disease was progressing. That only spurred me on harder to find another treatment, medicine, or solution to keeping him alive. I continued to push myself harder and harder, and the stress that I was putting myself through was incredible. But I never stopped to rest or give a second thought for myself. All my energy was for Dean.

When Dean and I first spoke to the oncologist and radiologist, I brought up the Ben Williams cocktail approach. The radiologist flat out refused to even discuss that method of treatment and said he had no knowledge of the author. The oncologist also said he had never heard of Ben Williams either; however, he was more compassionate and listened to my findings and suggested alternative treatment plan. At the time, I was astounded that neither doctor had heard of Ben Williams nor a cocktail approach to treatment. Whether it was from fear of litigation, big Pharma relationships, FDA approvals, or their ego—I didn't know. I realized that I was fighting more than brain cancer as an illness. I was fighting a broken system.

Do I have regrets? If I had known then what I know now, I would have skipped the radiation and chemo. Once Dean started the standard treatment, he was never the same. His quality of life was gone.

Pathology is the most important step one can get at time of initial resection. It is the key and map to solving the mystery of how to kill the tumor. Because if you do not know the genomic DNA of the tumor, you will not know how to fight it. There are clinical trials that will only take patients who have not had a craniotomy as well. By jumping into the doctor's protocol treatment and not using a *skilled* brain neurologist, your chances of survival drop dramatically. The first wrong step could be the catalyst on how successful treatment is.

If the hospital where you see your doctor does not offer certain treatment plans, they most likely will not even tell you about them. We limited ourselves by attending Group Health, which did not offer differing plans such as neuroablation, Gamma Knife or CyberKnife, or cocktail drug approach.

Only our oncologist recommended diet changes, naturopathic solutions, and alternative treatment. What's funny is, he was not originally from the United States, and he was one of the only doctors to encourage alternative care.

Once we started with the holistic doctor, we realized there were many other ways to boost the immune system versus tearing it down with chemo. In Dean's case, his body was his only defense, as the tumor could not be resected. His own immune system was his only hope. Currently, immunotherapy is one of the biggest advances in cancer.

I continued to research differing treatments, only scrapping them when they were unavailable or he was unqualified.

I wish I had gone with a different plan. I would have stuck with the naturopathic method and combined it with a targeted drug therapy or other alternative drugs based on his genomic markers. I would have insisted on a cocktail drug approach. I would have researched clinical trials. None of our doctors suggested them, and I didn't know enough about them to research myself. If your hospital facility does not offer certain drugs or therapies, they don't bother to tell you about them in most cases.

If Dean had even one good month of life left without the radiation, it would have been better than the poor quality of life he had left.

PULMONARY EMBOLISM TO STROKE

"You have a pulmonary embolism in your lungs," the doctor said. "I am very sorry."

"What does that mean?" I asked, confused and still in the dark about what Dean's prognosis meant.

The emergency room was starting to feel like a second home, we had been there more in the last four months than I had in my entire life. The on-call doctor had called for a CT scan of Dean's chest while I waited with him as he rested.

Excited that we were only a few days from leaving for Hawaii, I tried to keep Dean's spirits up by discussing all the things we were going to do once we got there.

Like a recurring nightmare, the doctor reentered Dean's room to deliver the bad news. "It means Dean will need to be admitted to the hospital for treatment."

"But how long will that take? We are leaving for vacation in a few days," I cried.

"Dean won't be able to travel for at least several weeks. This is very serious. I am finding him a room next door at Overlake Hospital. He will need to be admitted for a minimum of a week. They will need to regulate the blood clots and treat him with blood thinners," the doctor said.

I looked at Dean, who was stone-faced and staring straight ahead. I looked at the doctor, unable to keep the despair from my eyes.

He must not have had anything to add because he left us to digest this news and find Dean a room.

Dean and I reeled with disappointment yet again. *No, this can't be happening.* The thought of leaving was all Dean and I had looked forward to for weeks. It's what got him through the nightmare of radiation.

I was so pissed at this next unfair complication.

Why couldn't he get just a small fucking break? Why couldn't I?

I managed to hide my extreme disappointment from Dean, keeping my face blank, not wanting to make him feel worse. I knew he was as disappointed for me as I was for him.

"It's okay, baby," I told him. "What's important is that we are together and we are going to continue to fight until you feel better."

"I'm so sorry we can't go on vacation. I know how much you were looking forward to it. Thank you for taking care of me," he responded wearily.

"Of course. I love you. You are everything to me," I said, my eyes filling with tears as I walked over to give him a hug.

My heart bled for him. Even against this setback, he was thanking me and being sweet. I looked away so that he could not see my frustration, tears, and sadness. I felt horrible that once more, fucking cancer was taking away his quality of life in small increments, adding up to an all-consuming nightmare. I quickly found out that if Dean had not displayed the symptoms when he did, we would have gotten on the plane to Hawaii and he could have died instantly from a clot to the heart or brain. So, in a way, it was a blessing we found out before the plane trip.

I couldn't help thinking about how blissful our ignorance had been. Throughout the early days of treatment, Dean and I talked a lot about traveling. We had planned the trip to Hawaii for October, and as Dean came to the end of the initial radiation chemo combo, we celebrated, packing for our trip. He had not suffered from nausea or had a severe reaction to the chemo, so we counted our blessings. It didn't last, though. Before long, he needed a cane to walk. I noticed that as the radiation continued, Dean would start to drag his left foot when we went for hikes or walks. I attributed this quick decline of the left side to the radiation, not his tumor.

Going to Hawaii was supposed to be our reward for working so hard at recovery. We deserved a vacation, and we were going to lie in the sun, relax, and finally enjoy life a bit. It had been nonstop appoint-ments, surgery, radiation, and chemo since diagnosis. I calculated Dean would have three weeks to recuperate before we flew out.

What I didn't know, was that the forty-six days of treatment is just the initial blast to the brain when at its strongest. The real damage shows up *after* the radiologist completes the last two weeks of dosage. Dean's body and brain function continued to deteriorate once the treatment was over.

One day about two weeks after his sessions were complete, Dean was getting an IV at the holistic doctor and complained of a stabbing pain under his rib. The nurse stopped his IV and suggested that I take him to the hospital. I was hyperfocused on staying on schedule with work and all of his IV appointments, so I resented this change in plan. Dean was also angry and frustrated, and he did not want to go to the hospital either. We decided to go home and wait to see how he felt, but by the next day, Dean's condition had deteriorated, so I insisted that he let me take him to the hospital.

So here we were once again. Our disappointment so tangible I could almost reach out and touch it. My throat had a rock sitting between my tonsils, as I tried to keep it together one more time.

Dean was admitted into Overlake Hospital, and the pulmonary embolism doctor began treating him with blood thinners through an IV. He had to get the blood to a certain consistency of thinness for two days before he could release him to come home. The first day after Dean was admitted, I came in early in the morning to stay with him all day. When I walked into his room, there was a sign on the whiteboard that looked like the alphabet signs from when I was in kindergarten. On it were questions from the nursing staff for Dean, like his name and what he wanted to do after he got home. They had written his name at the top, but under the question "What do you like to do?" a nurse had written for him:

"To get better" and

"Go fly-fishing."

I don't know why, but this struck me so strongly, like Dean was my five-year-old son who was sick. It broke my heart that my strong, vibrant, sexy man was being reduced to a sign that reminded me of an assignment posted in a kindergarten class. I wanted to kiss him, hold him, and make him feel better. I wanted to take away all the angst and fear. I wanted so badly to fix everything. It was just so painful.

I sat down and asked him how he was doing.

"I'm good now that you're here," he said.

He was trying to sit up so that he could go to the bathroom. As I was helping him to stand, an alarm suddenly went off.

"What is that?" I asked him.

He shrugged that he didn't know. I went out to ask the nurses what was going on. One nurse in particular, a middle-aged blond woman, told me that Dean had been getting out of bed and wandering the halls at night and then getting lost. I remembered I had received a text from him during the night telling me he was lost and couldn't find his room. But when I had tried calling him back or texting, there was no response. *Wow,* I thought, *one more thing to worry about.* Again, I felt so bad for Dean. He was fast losing all of his short-term memory.

The estimated time to regulate the blood was seven days, but Dean wanted to go home so badly that I assured the PE doctor that I would continue treatment at home, and so they released him early—after only four days. I had to check in with the anticoagulation board daily until Dean's blood levels reached the recommended consistency to prevent clots. During this time, they had me giving him shots in the stomach and taking Warfarin pills. Dean never got off these injections, and not only were they very painful, the bruising on his stomach made it look like he'd been run over by a truck.

After four days of that at home, Dean started to get really sick again. He lost his desire to eat, he could barely walk, and he just generally wasn't feeling well. I knew something was really wrong. I begged him to have some breakfast. I told him I was going to have to take him back to the hospital if he didn't eat something. He was so desperate not to go back to the hospital that he forced down some eggs so I would not take him in. After I talked with the on-call nurse,

I decided he needed to go anyway. She said his symptoms were signs of either a brain bleed or tumor growth. Hearing that his brain might be bleeding, I couldn't take a chance. I promised Dean I would keep his stay as brief as possible. I just wanted to make sure he was okay.

He was not. The blood thinners had caused his brain to bleed, and he was having a stroke.

Once again, I did not fully understand what was happening to him. I did not know that a "brain bleed" was a stroke and that it was killing good brain cells. I did not understand that it was deadly. I was in shock with all the new and varying symptoms Dean was experiencing and was trying to make good choices concerning his care. He was so sick he didn't know what was going on either. Physically, he looked the same, but when the doctors asked him questions, he wasn't giving the correct answers.

Again, we went through questions like:

"Who is the President of the United States?"

"What year is it?"

I remember thinking, *Hmm, that's new,* when he answered Bush instead of Obama or 2005 instead of 2015. He'd known the right answer only the day before. Unfortunately, he ended up lying on that hard, uncomfortable gurney all day while they figured out how to get him downtown to Virginia Mason and find an available room. It was another long day of waiting and worrying. Finally, the ambulance came, and he seemed stable. I needed so badly to go home and sleep.

I asked Dean if he would be okay for a few hours, and he was jovial and upbeat.

"Sure, baby, please go home and get some rest," he assured me. He acted normal enough that I decided to take a few hours to sleep at home.

At 4:00 a.m. the next morning, I got up early to drive to Seattle. I hadn't slept much anyway, as I felt constant guilt if I wasn't with Dean night and day. When I arrived, I was told he had been taken to the ICU. I was just starting to wonder how serious it was. I quickly walked up to his room and couldn't believe my eyes. He was attached to several different machines and tubes.

"Baby?" I said tentatively. "How are you? Are you okay?"

He slowly turned his head, and the expression he gave me was as if he'd had a lobotomy.

He looked at me in a daze and gave me a slight smile.

What the hell? I thought.

"What have they done to you?" I demanded. "You were a little confused last night when I left you, but this morning you look like you are barely alive!"

He was unresponsive. The blank look on his face remained, and I immediately went to find a doctor.

His surgeon, Dr. L, came in the room not long after I returned. He stood over Dean and abruptly got to the point.

"What do you want me to save—the brain or the heart and lungs? The brain is bleeding from the blood thinners, but if we stop the thinners, he could have a pulmonary embolism."

I struggled to give him an answer. Dean's abrupt decline was mind-boggling to me.

"What do you mean?" I stammered, buying time to figure out what to do.

"He is in a position where he could die from the brain bleeding out, causing a massive stroke, or having a pulmonary embolism, which could also kill him," he replied.

"The doctor at the emergency yesterday already gave him Vitamin K to reverse the blood thinners to stop the bleeding," I informed him.

"Isn't there a way to stop the blood clots without the heavy blood thinners?" I asked.

I looked down at Dean's face while the surgeon and I were having this discussion. He looked stricken and shocked.

"That's it then? Am I just going to die?" he rasped.

My heart ached for him, and I racked my brain to figure a way out of this latest development.

"I want you to save his brain," I responded, thinking how insensitive it was to be discussing Dean's life looming over him while he lay helpless in the bed. I looked at the surgeon and motioned for him to follow me out of the room.

I murmured to Dean before I walked out.

"Don't worry, baby, I'm going to figure this out. I love you. Just rest."

The surgeon tried explaining that there was nothing he could do. Surgery was still out of the question. He walked me over to the MRI scan on the nurse's station computer to show me where the bleed was and explain that the likelihood that he would walk again was very low, possibly nonexistent. He then brought up hospice. I felt panicked and sad. I told him that I understood, but I refused to give up. I felt Dean's life slipping away from me as I tried desperately to hold on to it. He mentioned hospice more than once, and I finally started to think about it as a real possibility now that Dean was deteriorating so quickly.

The next doctor to come into Dean's room was a PE (pulmonary embolism) doctor. He explained that we should get on hospice but that he could put an IVC filter in his groin to stop the clots from moving up into the heart and lungs. *Why didn't they tell me this in the first place?* I wondered. I demanded to know why Dean was there in the hospital if there was nothing they could do.

"We are holding him for observation," he replied.

"Then I want to take him home today! What do I need to do to get him released?" I demanded.

I was angry. I didn't want Dean to die in that place, where they had tubes and bags sticking out of him everywhere and nurses that wouldn't leave him alone or let him sleep. The doctor immediately said he would assist me in any way to get Dean checked out that day. Also, he expedited hospice to contact me and immediately started the process of getting counselors and nurses to help treat Dean at home. I must say, I was impressed with how fast things progressed after that.

Luckily, Karly was there for moral support, and I called Dean's sister, Glenda, to come right away. I didn't know what was going to happen to him, and I knew that she wanted to be present if he were to die. She showed up at noon, having flown in from Sacramento.

Finally, at the end of the day, once they put the IVC filter in—a seven-minute procedure I felt they could have done before ever doing the blood thinners in the first place—we rolled Dean out to my car. We did not have a wheelchair, but the nurses who LOVED Dean said to just borrow one and bring it back later. They were very nice and helpful. The problem was that once we got home, we could not figure out how to get him up the front steps and into the house. It was all Glenda and I could do to lift the chair with him in it up those front steps. Luckily, he was able to roll into the master bedroom, which was on the main floor. Thank God I had called Glenda; she was my savior at that point in time. We prepared for the worst. Hospice delivered a special bed by the next day and sent medications out quickly.

Two days later, Dean was walking again. He seemed to be back to where he had been prior to the stroke.

Within four days he hit a wall, though, and his improvement stopped. As excited as we were to see that he could walk, a small piece of me knew it was the Dexamethasone, which they had increased to a higher dosage. I suspected it was giving us false hope. As time went on, Dean stopped improving physically, and the mental disabilities became more noticeable. The clots that had propagated in his legs were becoming occlusive. His legs—the left in particular—were very swollen, and all I could do was massage them and keep them elevated. Since it was too hard for him to walk, he couldn't get a lot of motion during the day to help with blood flow. If we went anywhere, I brought a wheelchair, as he could only walk about two minutes before needing to sit down.

It was very painful for him to stand because there was not enough oxygen getting to his veins. I would take time every day to massage Dean's legs to his feet a minimum of three times a day and wrap them tightly to help keep the swelling in check.

I felt utter hopelessness in the wake of Dean's stroke. He still would not talk about death or dying, and being unable to discuss these issues and come to terms with them was toxic to his system. I begged him to talk with a counselor. I arranged for ministers or counselors to meet with him, but he declined to open up to them. I was so frustrated because without his utter capitulation, how could he ever heal? That was one thing I could not fix. I became his twenty-four-hour nurse. He needed help for everything: showering, dressing, eating, and going to the bathroom. I despaired at his inability to get better and wondered if this would be our life indefinitely.

The holidays arrived, and I could see how emotionally hard they were on Dean. He knew that it would be his last Christmas, and it was his favorite time of year. Tia, my daughter, hosted Thanksgiving for me, and I was so grateful. The amount of work to cook the meal and clean while taking care of Dean was too much for me. He was still wheelchair bound, and he seemed to get overstimulated by all the kids and dogs.

I could see him getting angry over their playing and laughing after we had all sat down at the dinner table. I gave him a stern look that meant he should just ignore it because I knew he was about to explode and say something mean.

Then the dog started barking outside, and he finally snapped, "Can somebody shoot that dog?"

I looked at my nephew Colin, who was sitting next to him. We just looked at each other for a moment, frozen, then we quietly shared a laugh.

"Baby, someone will quiet the dog, but we aren't going to kill it," I gently told Dean with a smile.

He grunted and went back to eating, but I reflected on how different he had become. I realized that his illness was taking all of his bodily energy to survive, and any extra stimulation was irritating him. He was focused inward, in pain, and no longer fully connected to reality.

As Christmas approached, I forced myself to decorate. It was an overwhelming task even on a good year, let alone during Dean's full-time care. I knew it would most likely be his last holiday, so Karly, Matt, and I took him to the local tree farm to cut down a tree. He was having a good day and managed to use his cane to walk to the edge of the trees to pick one out. He found a perfect Noble Fir, and we strapped it in the truck and set it up at home. He watched Karly and I decorate it, and I caught his face, tears glistening on his cheeks, staring at the tree all lit up at night. His sadness was palpable. I could not help feeling depressed as well, trying to emotionally put myself in his shoes. What would it feel like to have this be my last Christmas? I couldn't fathom it.

Waking up Christmas morning was anticlimactic. There was always a bit of excitement, but this year we both lacked our inner childish joy. I felt Dean was going through the motions with the weight of certain death looming over his head, and early-morning presents and sweets did little to change how meaningless it all felt.

As time went on, I realized Dean really only wanted to make it through the holidays. After the New Year, he gave up. He started fighting the medications and treatments in full force. I pulled him off the Valcyte—an antiviral drug used to treat HIV patients that has some success with GBM patients—to put him on another drug called Tarceva, a small lung cancer medication that also has success with GBM patients.

Unfortunately, this drug was not an approved medication by the insurance company, and they would not cover the prescription for his illness without further proof of why it was needed. That medication cost $9,000 for a thirty-day supply. I tried to send articles and justification through the Swedish program, but Regence insurance flat out denied it. I wish now I had left him on the Valcyte. The tumor was holding steady until that point, and there was no new growth. We figured we were doing something right. I was looking for anything to have a bigger impact to help him. The battle became keeping his body functioning, and treating the tumor went on the back burner by January. He was so miserable being unable to walk, but by February, we were able to put him on a different blood thinner.

Slowly, Dean started to stand and move with a cane or walker again. He appeared to be getting stronger, and I enrolled him in physical therapy. He was walking much better and starting to recover from some of the neuro deficits. During that time, I was slowly reducing the Dexamethasone until he was down to 8 mg. It was thinning his skin, and his legs and his arm muscles were severely atrophied. He also lost a lot of his vision and could no longer read. I was focused on getting him off of it so that he could get stronger, but this proved to be a big mistake. At that same time, his current oncologist wanted to lower the Dexamethasone dosage as well, as he had seen Dean's improvement. He had me reduce the dosage by 2 mg. Up until that point, I had been reducing it by a half to one milligram per week. I thought 2 mg was pretty aggressive, but he was doing so well that I thought it couldn't hurt to try. I could always up the dosage if needed.

When I lowered Dean's dose to 6 mg, within three days he had regressed to barely walking to the bathroom. Dean and his doctor wanted to stay the course, so I continued to hold him at the same amount. By the end of the week, Dean started to suffer from horrific headaches. It got so bad that I rushed him to the emergency room one morning. He was moaning in agony, and the morphine wasn't working. The emergency oncologist on call wanted me to up the Dexamethasone dosage back to 10 mg. I insisted on talking with his oncologist, who was unavailable. I ended up taking Dean home and giving him stronger morphine pills instead. This caused further complications of stopping up his colon and created painful bowel movements. After only one more day, I gave in and reluctantly upped the Dexamethasone back to 8 mg and then 10 mg to get the headaches under control.

What I figured out was that the Dexamethasone was controlling the headaches, and I had gone under the threshold. It was reducing the swelling of the tumor. When I went below the threshold of the steroid's ability to keep the swelling down, his headaches increased dramatically.

That is why I called using Dexamethasone "making a deal with the devil." It bought us time but ultimately contributed to killing Dean's body.

By mid-February, Dean had his first big fall, and after that he was never the same. One night when he was still able to use his cane, he got up to go to the bathroom. In his disorientation of waking in the middle of the night, he fell and hit his head on the corner of the nightstand then fell into the wall and tore up his arms. The loud thud startled me awake, and with my heart pounding in my ears, I jumped up to help him. He had fallen in between the bed and the nightstand where I could not get leverage to lift him. I ended up pulling and dragging him out of the narrow area by his feet. He was angry and scared, and I could not lift him back up to the bed. There was blood everywhere, and I tried to clean him up while calling the neighbor next door to see if he could come help me put Dean back in bed.

Luckily, he answered his phone at 4:00 a.m. and came right over. Dean was frightened, humiliated, and discouraged yet again that he could not walk. His bruised and purple arms were torn in all different places, and I tried to bandage up the open wounds as fast as I could. It was all the neighbor and I could do to lift him back on the bed. Dean was a big man at 6'1", and at dead weight he not easy to pick up.

He never really walked again after that event. I don't know if I was just hopeful or blind, but I did not recognize the signs that he was dying. They were all there: the lack of appetite, the non-interest in treatment and medication, and the inability to walk or function daily.

Dean's attitude became very negative at that point. I had all these emotions every day during the struggle to help him live; I felt like I was drowning in despair and slowly sinking into a pit of depression. My emotions ranged from hope and happiness to frustration, anger, sadness, and depression nearly every hour. At night, I would grieve in private for the loss of what life used to be, and the man who had been, my husband, best friend, and lover. Even though he was not gone, he was different. Then I would feel guilty for feeling sad. I was lucky he was still with me. I felt he was still alive because of my sheer will for him to live. I had put hours into research, holistic care, hospitals, radiation/chemo, supplements, counseling, ozone therapy, speech therapy, and physical therapy. Yet I felt like my body was fracturing apart.

Had it become my battle and not his? Was I fighting to the death of me and not him? Because I felt he was unable to make rational decisions, had I taken his life upon myself to save? In my moments of darkness, I felt I could not continue another day. When should I have stopped and let happen what would happen? How would I learn to accept it?

I wished Dean wanted to do what was necessary to help himself live as much as I wanted him to live. I wished he didn't have that god-awful tumor. I wished for my life to be the way it was before. I wished I had never heard of cancer.

SECOND OPINIONS

As with most people diagnosed with a terminal illness, protocol from doctors and family is to get a second opinion. So, with some hope, I researched where to take Dean for another diagnosis. I had found some information on a procedure called NeuroBlate and was desperately trying to find a doctor who would do this procedure on Dean.

Basically, they insert a rod into the brain and heat the tumor from inside, which is supposed to kill the cancer. This procedure has little downtime and is not painful to the patient. Unfortunately, no one performs this procedure in the state of Washington. Also, medical insurance will not cross state lines, and the procedure costs upward of $250,000.

I made an appointment with a top neurosurgeon at the University of Washington, based on a recommendation from my brother-in-law, Mike, who coincidently also had a glioma removed seven years earlier. His was a Grade II and was caught early on and in a right lobe location that caused him no deficits when removed. This surgeon at UW had a good reputation and had done many, many surgeries of this kind. My sister and I were in awe that we both married men who had brain tumors. What were the odds?

Dean and I arrived at the University of Washington one hot August summer morning with some hope and anticipation of hearing good news. We were led back to the small exam rooms and told to have a seat by the attending nurse.

Suddenly, the surgeon strode into the room with a woman trailing behind. He did not introduce himself or the woman, and I wasn't even sure why she was there. He quickly sat down and demanded, "So, why are you here?"

I was a little taken aback at his rudeness, and Dean and I nervously looked at each other. I thought to myself, *Wow, he didn't even introduce himself or say hello.*"

"We came for a second opinion on Dean's brain tumor," I tentatively spoke up. "I brought his latest MRIs for your review."

"The scans were forwarded to me by your current oncologist, and I have already reviewed them. There is nothing we can do," he said arrogantly. "Surgery is not an option. Haven't you already been told this?"

"We thought maybe you might be able to operate and resect some of the tumor."

He abruptly said, "We cannot operate. There is nothing to be done. You're looking at a lifespan of six to nine months."

The shock of his callousness and insensitivity caused me to tear up. I felt frozen in hurt and despair, and I could hardly speak over the lump in the back of my throat. During this conversation, Dean was silent. I grasped for any ideas to present but could not think clearly due to the tone of the conversation. I had never encountered a doctor so lacking in compassion. His abruptness was disconcerting, and it threw me off my ability to think of the questions I had wanted to ask.

I finally was able to tearfully ask, "How about any clinical trials?"

"You don't have medical insurance to cover any procedures here at UW, but I can see if I can get someone in our clinical trials department to speak with you today. You may have to wait."

I could not believe how discouraging and cold he was.

We sat in awkward silence for a moment, and suddenly I couldn't breathe. I wanted to be away from that man immediately.

"That's okay," I said. "We will discuss whether a clinical trial is the right thing for us."

He quickly stood up and, with hardly a glance our way, left the room with his young associate right behind him.

No "Nice to meet you," "Sorry," or "Have a good day." He just walked out.

Dean and I left the room just as quickly. We looked at each other when we got to the elevators, and I knew he felt the exact same way I did.

"That guy was the biggest asshole I have ever met," I said, and Dean wholeheartedly agreed.

We were solemn as we got into the elevators, contemplating what had just happened. I could feel our spirits binding together to block this unpleasant experience, and we both tried to shed the cloak of the negativity the surgeon had spewed on us.

In the past, I had read stories of others who were diagnosed with a grave illness and had a bad experience with a doctor during their initial exam, and that one was definitely ours. Since Dean's tumor was inoperable, that surgeon didn't care. He could do nothing; therefore, he wanted nothing to do with us. He did not care about Dean, nor did he care about being kind.

Later when Dean was a lot sicker and had already had the stroke, we went to see another doctor at the Seattle Cancer Care Alliance. He was not a surgeon; we had learned our lesson that type of doctor was of no help, so we went to see a neuro-oncologist. This doctor was much more helpful and sat and discussed with us at length Dean's diagnosis. He was the one who finally explained why Dean's tumor could not be operated on, injected with a virus, or heated up via neuroablation technique. Why had we not seen a BRAIN SPECIALIST in the first place? This was another lesson I learned halfway into the journey.

The doctor explained with pictures and detailed explanations that the location of Dean's tumor within his brain was crossing the corpus callosum, which is both globes of the brain. Once a tumor does that, it compromises the brain's ability to communicate from globe to globe. Dean's tumor was a primary tumor, which means it grew within itself. It was not an encapsulated malignant ball, it was cancer cells that had overgrown and overtaken good cells in one area of the brain. There were still good pathways that communicated to each other. By cutting the tumor out, or killing that large area with neuroablation or other methods, it would remove or kill the entire area in which the brain functioned together as a whole and would have similar results to a lobotomy. He would not be able to talk or communicate. It would most likely affect his left-side motor skills as well. His entire quality of life would be gone.

With that explanation, I finally understood what the other surgeons had been unable to explain to me. The only way to save Dean was to shrink the tumor or have his own body fight off the advancement of further cancer cells.

The neuro-oncologist recommended the Optune device and wanted us to start the chemotherapy again. He thought Dean was strong enough for it.

The Optune device is a machine that you attach to your head with electrodes. It emits sound waves that have shown to reduce growth of tumors. Some patients take the Temodar (chemo) while wearing the device for more positive results. Unfortunately, Dean would have to shave his head every couple of days so the nodes could stick to his scalp. This could have caused extreme skin sensitivity, as he would have to wear this unit twenty-three hours a day for it to work. He would also have to wear a backpack every day to carry the machine around. Dean did not even want to try it. I think he would have had skin issues. Years back, he had to wear a heart monitor for two days, and his skin was so sensitive that he developed huge red welts everywhere the nodes stuck to his chest. He could barely wear it for the recommended forty-eight hours, as the rash was too painful and inflamed wherever the nodes attached to his chest.

And more chemo? I didn't know. He did so poorly every time we gave it to him. Not to mention the blood clots and swelling. This was my dilemma. Should I prolong life just to keep my husband alive, or should I consider quality of life? He had no quality of life, and I didn't know it then, but I was already fighting a losing battle. Dean was fast losing his will to live, and I was still fighting for the both of us. At this point, he really started resisting me on treatments and medications. He was no longer interested.

PRE-GRIEF

I heard a *clunk ... clunk ... clunk* coming down the hall toward the office.

"Hey, baby, how are you doing? You have been so quiet." I looked up from my computer because Dean had hobbled down the hall from the living room using his cane.

He looked at me with such despair. There were tears in his eyes, and I felt panic that there was something terribly wrong. I still could not get used to seeing my formerly stoic, strong husband weep in front of me.

"Do you know what the worst part is?" he asked gently.

"What?" I said, though I honestly didn't want to know what he was referring to. It all just hurt too much.

"That I will miss you," he whispered.

"What do you mean?" I pretended not to understand what he was talking about to buy time to work up a positive response.

"When I'm gone," he said simply. "I won't get to spend time with you every day, go places, and have fun." Then Dean cried harder.

I started to cry as well, and I jumped up to give him a long hug.

"Look at me!" I reached out and turned his face to mine. "You will be in heaven—happy, healthy, and whole. I am the one who will be left behind. It's me that will miss you more." I earnestly bored my eyes into his so that he would understand.

We held on tight to each other for a while and then broke away. Nothing else could be said. I could not bring myself to give him false words of encouragement. Our emotions were too raw.

Dean cried a lot in those days—not once, but many times throughout the day—and it was one of the hardest parts of his illness for me to bear. His inability to communicate his fear, frustration, and sadness came out in the number of tears he shed. It broke my heart every time he wept. I could not remember seeing Dean cry more than a couple of times in the past twelve years. As his body gave out a little more every day, on the surface he was stoic, brave, and accepting. But inside, he was emasculated and frustrated. It wore down his will to live.

Dean hated that I had to help him with every need. He had lost his role as my husband. We grieved together in some ways but separately for the individual things we could not share. I admired his bravery every moment. I would have been terrified to face every treatment, drug, and symptom of his illness. He was not ready for death, and neither was I. He was terrified, but he hid it from everyone, including me.

I realized that he was trying to spare me from his fears, emotions I could not understand as he experienced them.

After his diagnosis, we spent every minute together. We both lived and breathed each other every moment. He was still the most exciting person I wanted to talk to every day. We loved each other more as time progressed, even as he became sicker. In a sad way, his brain tumor brought us even closer because we were clinging to each other, fighting for life on a sea of imminent death.

I know that Dean *hated* that I worked so hard every day. He felt so bad that I had to take care of all his needs along with running the company. A part of me knew the reason he gave up his will to live was because he did not want me to have to take care of him. He constantly apologized for everything I did for him. I would reassure him that I didn't mind, especially when it came to anything to do with going to the bathroom.

Despite my love for Dean, the days and nights were exhausting. I tried not to think how long I could handle the twenty-four-hour care for an extended period of time. I would be frustrated with myself.

"He is dying," I would tell myself. "You have no right to feel bad for yourself."

I knew he could feel my sadness and frustration, but I would not tell him how I felt because I wanted to protect his feelings. He did not get that option. He had to suffer the indignities of his illness along with expressing all his needs. He was dependent on me in every way.

While I suffered the grief of slowly losing the man who was my everything, he suffered the loss of being the superman to take care of me, our sexual intimacy, and his quality of life. All the things that made him feel needed and happy were slowly stripped from his life in layers, as the treatment plan and brain cancer robbed him unforgivably. All of that happened so quickly that it never registered in my mind that his life was almost gone. I hadn't begun to feel the pain of loss at that point. We both reeled so much every day from his ever-changing physical and mental loss that it was hard to comprehend where we started from.

Even as poorly as Dean felt, we both denied that the grim reaper was at the door. We had not even entertained the idea of grieving his death.

DISNEYLAND

Throughout Dean's illness, he constantly brought up going on a trip, getting out of town, or just leaving home for a few days. When we had to cancel the Hawaii trip in October, I continued to hope that he would stabilize long enough to travel. I felt so guilty, as I couldn't fathom taking him anywhere far from his doctors or the hospital.

He would always say, "Let's go to Alaska and go fishing," or "Let's take off to Hawaii, where it's hot and sunny."

I would nod and agree with a vague, noncommittal response. "Oh, sure. Let's see how it goes, and I will check into it."

I did not want to take that hope from him by refuting his physical ability to go, but I had to battle my fear that I couldn't handle travel with him by myself. Since the pulmonary embolism situation, I was doubly scared of flying with him.

I knew I was terrified of taking on the task of arranging and executing a vacation with him, in addition to all the full-time care and chores I had. I was overwhelmed with work, medical appointments, dispensing medications, and handling Dean's general twenty-four-hour care. How would I ever be able to get someone to run the business if I were gone? On top of that, how would I schedule the trip, pack our bags, organize medications, arrange for a rental car, check bags at the airport, and figure out how to mobilize him in a wheelchair by myself? I had chronic guilt over not being able to help Dean do everything he wanted before he died. In early January, I talked with my sister and finally planned a trip to Disneyland in late February and early March, and she agreed to accompany us. I didn't want to plan it too early in the year because it might be cold in Los Angeles in January, and I wanted Dean to enjoy the sun. Dean loved the sun and cherished the warm days anywhere. It was a gamble, though, because I did not know how he would be doing by then.

In early February, he had been doing great. He was in physical therapy and back to seeing a speech therapist. He was walking with a cane and only needing the wheelchair for long-distance walks. I had him on Ozone Therapy—a way to infuse oxygen into his body via his ears, using an oxygen tank, Ozone regulator, and tubing—and it really seemed to help him cognitively and physically. I was so excited because it felt like he was getting better; all of his treatments seemed to be working. As I mentioned in an earlier chapter, all his improvements halted after reducing the steroid drug Dexamethasone. Those events happened two weeks prior to our trip to Disneyland. Due to his deterioration, physically and mentally, he was losing his will to fight for life and started to express anxiety over traveling. It wasn't until about a week before we were scheduled to leave that he brought up his concern.

"Maybe we should cancel the upcoming trip to California," he told me hesitantly.

I responded with anger because I didn't want him to give up.

"My sister and I went to a lot of trouble and money to schedule this trip for you. Not to mention your sister Glenda is meeting us there as well. Please don't give up until after we get back from this trip. You have to at least try until then." I pleaded with him.

"But what if the travel is just too much for me?"

In that comment, I knew there was so much more he wasn't saying. He was uncertain and scared of going out of his comfort zone, but I was hoping Dean's will to live would return. I wanted him to feel renewed energy after having fun in California.

He agreed to go, albeit reluctantly, but I think he knew how important it was to me. He was trying to make me happy even in with his daily mental and physical discomfort. I loved him so much for that. I remained hopeful that Dean would change his mind about the medications and treatments and things would start to get better again. But with his latest setback, it was hard for him to rebound back to the hope he'd had a week before.

The plane ride was an event in itself. I had a whole new appreciation for people with disabilities. When someone has a disability that prevents them from standing, walking, or lifting themselves, they must rely on others to help them in the environment of an airplane. While these assistants are just trying to help, people with disabilities may still feel less than whole in such situations. This was certainly true for Dean. He'd lost his independence, and it took two airline employees to lift him onto the modified wheelchair that airports use to move down the narrow aisle and to put him in his seat. I did not know how I would get him to a bathroom midflight if he needed to go. Luckily, he did not have to go while in the air. That was a stress and concern for him, but he managed to hold it while flying. The flight was only two and a half hours at most, so as soon as we got off the plane, I took him to the nearest restroom.

Even though Dean was first on the plane, he was the last one off. We had to wait for all other passengers to disembark, then for the helpers to bring the modified wheelchair to load him, wheel him off the plane, and reload him into the wheelchair we brought from home. It was time consuming and embarrassing for Dean. Another indignity endured from shitty brain cancer.

We arrived in LA on schedule and met up with Glenda. Lisa hustled us to the nearest shuttle area so we could pick up our rental car. Finally, an Enterprise bus showed up, and luckily, it had one of those wheelchair hoists that hydraulically lifted Dean's chair into the van. We loaded all the suitcases and drove thirty minutes to the nearest service center.

By the time we got our car, loaded the luggage, and arrived at the Airbnb house we rented, Dean and I were drained. I wheeled him into the house so we could tour the place. He could not even stand up at that point. He was also having constipation issues from the morphine, and Lisa and Glenda witnessed a meltdown he had while I tried to help him go to the bathroom. For most of the trip, Dean was the most irritable I had ever experienced since his initial diagnosis. I realized he was anxious being in unknown territory away from home. He lashed out at me and Glenda as we tried to help him. I think he was acting unnaturally because he was uncomfortable, scared, and in pain.

At the time, I was too overwhelmed to understand his emotions. My hormones had been going crazy from premenopause, and I was not sleeping. In addition, I would set my alarm for 5:00 every morning to make sure he got some sort of pain medication for the day, so he did not wake up with a migraine. Also, he would have to go to the bathroom every night—sometimes several times a night. It was always an ordeal to bring the wheelchair up to the bed, lock it in, help him stand and sit into the chair, reset the foot pegs and lock them in, and finally wheel him to the toilet. By the time he was finished and I had wheeled him back to bed, I would be wide awake. I might have just gotten back to sleep, and it would start all over again. This went on night after night, and eventually it was hard for me to function during the day. I found myself falling asleep sitting up I was so tired.

We settled into our temporary home and excitedly planned the next few days of our adventure. Dean was trying very hard to have a good time. I didn't realize it, but his headaches were constant, and the pain was worse than he was telling me. I should have intuitively known that he was not feeling well, but not insisting that he be honest with me may have been my way to avoid understanding that he had become sicker. And in my distracted state, I did not recognize that he was really suffering.

The house was nice and spread out. It had a big pool and a hot tub. I could not get Dean to try either one—another sign I should have noticed that he really was not feeling well. Each day, he would sit out by the pool and watch us three girls swim or lay in the sun. He just hung out, not really engaging too much with what we were all doing, lost in his own world. It was only in the seventies, not too hot, but he soaked up every bit of sunshine he could. His habit of sitting for hours doing nothing was just so strange to me since he had been such an ambitious and busy person before his diagnosis. It was just another way the tumor was taking over his brain and his body was failing.

The second day in LA, we all drove to Disneyland. Dean was chipper, and we were all excited to hit the rides and see the park. The first ride we all went on was the Test Track in Disney's California

Adventure. Dean was laughing out loud and enjoying that ride a lot. It was so good to see him having fun and smiling. We actually had a great time the entire day with only one exception. The open cuts on Dean's arm from when he fell that night in our bedroom two weeks before would not heal. For some random reason, they all decided to bleed at once. I had brought Band-Aids in case he needed them, and we ended up going through all of those until we ran out. We headed to the First Aid Station at Disneyland, but they were not much help. I was able to get a couple of makeshift compresses from their first aid office, but Dean was going through boxes, and it was alarming how much the wounds were bleeding. We finally left the park early and went back to the house. We pulled all the dressings off his arms, and he sat in the sun for several hours. After that, they finally started healing by the next day.

We took the next day off and hung out by the pool all day. I think Dean really enjoyed this, as we had no agenda and he could just relax as much as possible. Our second day at Disneyland did not fare as well as the first. That time, we were in Main Street, U.S.A. We decided to ride the roller coaster Big Thunder Mountain Railroad. In the past, Dean loved roller coasters. There was not a roller coaster he would not go on, so I didn't think twice about taking him on that ride. As we waited in line, Lisa, Glenda, and I strategized on how to quickly load and unload him from the seat. They only give you thirty seconds to load and strap in. We waited in line for an hour and then finally pushed his wheelchair up to the designated area. The car pulled up, and we all jumped into action. Dean was almost unable to stand, so we all positioned ourselves and hoisted and pulled him into the car. I buckled his seatbelt for him in the front seat with me, and off we went. The ride was very jerky and fast, and I knew immediately that it was a bad idea for Dean to go on this ride. He was trying to hold on, but his hands were slippery with sweat. He was silent but leaning into me as the car on the rails jerked, swayed, and flew around the corners. I was laughing when I glanced over at him and noticed that he looked very pale and scared. I was so worried about him that I lost all enjoyment and continued to keep an eye on him to make sure he was okay until the ride was over.

Finally, it came to a quick halt, and we all jumped back into action to help him up. As they brought his wheelchair over, I literally tried to lift him completely out of the seat by myself in an effort to hurry when all of a sudden, my back popped.

"Oh shit ... Noooo!" I thought, *This can't be happening.*

I had just thrown my back out. I screamed for Lisa to come help me as she and Glenda got Dean into the chair. I hobbled bent over out of my seat and made it to the closest railing.

"You guys, I just threw my back out! What am I going to do now?" I wailed.

"Come sit down." Lisa said as she guided me over to a nearby wooden bench.

She calmed me down, and we slowly made our way out of the ride area. I could not stand upright and had to walk hunched over until we found a bench to sit on. Luckily, Lisa had some painkillers, and I was able to take those so I could at least get around. Glenda took over pushing Dean in the wheelchair. I was pushing myself to exhaustion, and my body was finally showing signs of breaking down.

"I didn't like that ride, and I don't want to do any more of those," Dean said.

"I know, baby," I told him. "I could tell you were very upset. I'm really sorry, I didn't think about how fast and jerky it was going to be."

I was thinking the speed of the car made his head dizzy. Imagine going on a fast roller coaster after taking meds for a migraine. I'm sure that is what he experienced. Poor guy. I felt so bad for him. Another pleasure taken from him. *Will he ever get back to normal?* I asked myself.

The rest of the trip was uneventful. We lay by the pool, went shopping, and ate out in local restaurants. Dean had fun but was eager to get home. Because I was so close to him, and in denial, I could not see that he was becoming very indisposed. This was not a reaction to illness, medication, or exhaustion, but the sickness of approaching death. One major sign was that his hands were always wet with sweat. Later I found out that is a symptom of the body preparing to die.

The trip home was similar to the first airplane ride—long, exhausting, and requiring us to go through the seating ordeal again. When I see people with disabilities now, I always make sure I assist in any way I can. You don't realize how many places are not set up to accommodate wheelchairs.

When we got home, Dean was so happy to be there. He was loving and supportive again and grateful to be home. I guess the travel was not all that he hoped in his incapacitated state. I think he realized he couldn't run away from his pain.

FLY-FISHING

"Good morning, baby! It's time to get dressed," I said in a singsong voice to wake Dean up gently.

"It's fly-fishing day today! Aren't you excited?" I enthused as I could see he was grumpier than normal this morning.

"Lewis is coming to pick you up soon, and you get to go on a guided trip today!"

"Okay," he answered quietly as he tried to sit up.

I bustled around, getting his clothes together and putting his pills gingerly by the nightstand. At this point, he would get mad when I brought him his medication, as he no longer wanted to swallow so many supplements.

"Ouch!" he cried out as I tried to put his compression socks on. "It really hurts!"

"I don't understand why it's so hard to get these on today." Still, I pushed and pulled and managed to get them both on.

I could see Dean was in pain.

"Does it hurt still?" I asked.

"Yes, its uncomfortable on this right leg." He grimaced at me.

"You know what? I'm just going to leave this one off." I pulled the sock off his right leg quickly and finished dressing him in his fishing clothes.

He mumbled, "Maybe I shouldn't go today?"

"Oh, baby, this may be your last chance to go fishing for a while," I encouraged. "Lewis has it all set up with a guide, and the day's events are paid for. Are you sure?"

He looked thoughtful but worried and said, "I guess I could go."

"Great! I'm sure you are going to have so much fun! It's a beautiful day, and I don't know when you will get to go again for a while."

I had set up a fishing trip for Dean with a man we did business with in asphalt. Lewis came into our lives through partnering on business projects and wanted to joint venture some of the work we did. He was very similar to Dean in that they were the same age, both loved fly-fishing, and owned their own asphalt business. Lewis had been wanting to take Dean fishing for several months, but about the time he initially approached me about a day trip, Dean had just suffered the stroke. When he came back to me several months later, I told him that it was now or never. Dean had overall declined at that point but would still have a somewhat decent day here and there.

Riding the roller coaster of GBM was difficult and confusing. Somehow the body rallies randomly, and because it would take me by surprise, I would hope that Dean was improving. The hope never went away, and the daily physical changes continued to confuse me enough that I thought his health was getting better. I'd woken up that Saturday morning feeling excited to get Dean ready to go on his big trip. I was still waking up every day at 5:00 a.m. to give him either the cannabis or morphine to ward off the headaches he was now getting first thing in the morning.

I, too, was looking forward to Dean leaving for the day, as I had painters scheduled to come in and paint the bedroom and living room. I wanted it all to be done before he came home so he wasn't inconvenienced. Plus, I was worried about the paint smell making him sick.

Lewis showed up, and we decided to put Dean in the back seat of the pickup so he could stretch out his leg. We had to lift him up on the edge and scoot him toward the other passenger door so his back was resting along the window. The truck was a king cab and not a crew cab, so the room was already limited. The truck was very dirty as well, and as I shut the door I looked at Dean one last time. His left hand was palm out, with the fingers curled inward, and his arm was bent at the elbow, shaking uncontrollably. His face had a look of pain, fear, and concern. I closed the door and took a breath.

Am I doing the right thing? I asked myself. I felt like I was making him go. I questioned my every decision, feeling so alone and guilty.

I didn't know what to do, so I let events just continue forward, and after Lewis threw the wheelchair in the back of the truck, they drove off. I asked Lewis to give Dean his medication, which I sent in Dean's bag. I was worried like a mother over her baby boy going off to the first day of school.

He's a grown man, I told myself.

If he really didn't want to go, he would have been more adamant. *Let him live ... Let him go!* Later I got a text from Lewis that said Dean was doing fine, and they had arrived and were getting in the boat.

"Great!" I sighed with relief.

I released myself from guilt and confirmed that I had done the right thing. Dean would have a great day, and I could relax and enjoy the little freedom for a few hours.

The day went by quickly, and the painters I hired to paint the bedroom and living room finished. I was able to put all the furniture back and restore order to the house. Before I knew it, Dean and Lewis were pulling into the driveway. I ran out to help unload Dean from the truck and see how he was doing. Luckily, Chad—our son-in-law—was visiting and able to help Lewis get him out of the truck and into his wheelchair. It took all three of us to get Dean out of the truck and into the house. I could see that he was in extreme pain from his leg, as he cried out every time he was jostled too much.

I called hospice immediately and spoke with the answering attendant. "I need a doctor to come out right away."

By that time, it was about 7:00 on a Saturday night. The hospice answering service asked me the usual questions to determine if Dean really needed a site visit. I told them that I thought he had an infection in his leg due to the fluid buildup and blood clots. I thought he needed antibiotics.

"Okay, we will dispatch a nurse as soon as we can," the attendant replied.

An hour and a half later, I got a call from the on-call hospice doctor. "I couldn't find your home, and I have been driving around for over an hour," she said.

We went over the directions several times. Her phone kept dropping the call, and it took several calls to finally figure out she had the wrong address. By that time, two hours had passed, and I was getting really mad. I knew Dean was in a lot of pain, and I wanted him to get help as soon as possible.

I called the main line again and told them that the nurse had not arrived and asked what was happening. They apologized and said that the nurse that called me went home because it went over her shift after she lost time with the wrong address. They would be sending out another doctor, but she was in Seattle, so it would be an hour before she got there.

"Well, please ask her to hurry. My husband is in pain," was all I could say. What could I do?

Finally, three hours after I had made the initial call, the on-call nurse arrived. She was a small older woman who seemed nice but somewhat scattered. She took one look at Dean's leg and said he needed to go to the hospital.

"WHAT?" I barked. "I thought everyone was treated at home. Isn't that the point of being on hospice?"

I knew Dean would hate going to the hospital.

She replied, "We can't determine what the infection is here, and only the hospital can treat him with the antibiotics he needs."

I was so pissed off and tired from the extremely long day. It was now past 10:00 p.m.

"If he has to go, then how do we load him in my car? You and I can't lift him, and he is in extreme pain," I told her.

She replied, "I will call an ambulance to come and pick him up. What facility should we take him to?"

I was frantically looking online to see what hospital would be best.

She came to look over my shoulder at the computer and asked, "Where is the nearest facility?"

"Valley Medical Center," I said, "but I don't want him to go there. I have heard bad things about it."

Because I was so tired and felt overwhelmed and worried about Dean, I did not even think about the new hospital he was seeing his oncologist at, Swedish in Issaquah. I just couldn't think. I suggested Overlake in Bellevue. She quickly agreed and made the calls for the ambulance to come pick Dean up. The ambulance finally showed up around 11:30 p.m. By that time, I was full of anxiety and so tired I knew I wasn't going to be able to drive an hour and sit up all night. Dean was scared and in pain but resting somewhat. They loaded him onto the gurney, and I called my brother-in-law, Mike.

"Can you please meet the ambulance at Overlake Hospital?" I asked him. "Just give me two to three hours to sleep, and I will meet you there." Mike and Lisa only lived five minutes from the facility.

"Sure, no problem," he agreed. He said he would let me know when Dean got there and how he was doing. I almost wilted with relief. I had a couple of hours reprieve to get some rest and get my head on straight.

Early the next morning when I arrived, Dean was almost out of his head in pain. He was moaning and throwing his arm over his face every two minutes. They had put the IV in the arm he kept moving, so I would sit by him and gently lower his arm every couple of minutes to stop the IV from pinching his skin. They had started him on some antibiotics, but his pain was so great that they gave him Dilaudid (a pain medication similar to morphine) to help him rest more comfortably.

I received a phone call by midmorning from hospice telling me that Dean was in a hospital that was not approved by the Providence Hospice program. I asked how this happened, as the hospice nurse the night before had helped me to pick out which hospital to send him to by ambulance. They did not know but said they would work to rectify the mistake. Unfortunately, this meant he needed to be moved again in his weakened state. Talk about piling more stress on me and giving me something else to figure out. Luckily, they worked quickly and sent an ambulance to pick him up later that evening, and he was set up in his new room at Swedish Hospital in Issaquah by 7:00 p.m. That decision to send him to the wrong hospital was a testament to how poorly I was thinking, as that was where his oncologist resided and where he had been treated. It was a new facility, and I just did not think about it being a hospital. This mistake cost me more than inconvenience, I incurred additional hospital expenses as well. I berated myself, hitting my forehead with the butt of my hand, chanting *dumb ... dumb ... dumb.*

Luckily, he seemed to be improving by that evening and was resting more comfortably. I made the decision to go home and get some rest after 10:00 p.m. but arranged to have my brother-in-law there early the next morning so Dean would not be alone too long. I arrived by 8:00 the next morning, and again, he seemed to be doing incrementally better.

By now, it was Monday morning, and I was back to running the company in between making decisions about Dean's healthcare and answering emails and phone calls. By Tuesday he was doing even better; he was sitting up and joking, eating somewhat, and resting comfortably. I never considered that he wouldn't get through the latest setback. It was just a leg infection. The antibiotics were helping him to improve every day, albeit through a lot of pain. It was diagnosed as cellulitis, which I discovered through research was a very painful condition. I still thought that it was just a curable infection, and since it was Tuesday, Karly was coming to spend the afternoon with Dean so I could steal away to get payroll and taxes paid for business and get some rest.

I came back in the next morning. While I was away, the hospice doctor had insisted on giving Dean an enema and laxatives, as he had been on the painkillers, and his bowels would be impacted. Dean was moaning in agony when I walked in, and the usual SWAT team of nurses were present, rolling him from side to side, and picking him up with a hoist to clean up the poop that he had no control of running out of him. He was crying out in pain and embarrassment. Even in his somewhat unresponsive state, he was distressed to be going to the bathroom in his bed. The cellulitis was still agony if touched, and every time they cleaned him up, it caused him endless misery. Due to their policy that a patient needed to be turned every hour to avoid bedsores, Dean suffered needlessly for several days, until they decided it wasn't necessary anymore.

I stopped abruptly in the doorway and recoiled from his latest torture. I simultaneously cringed and felt shame that I was shying away from his pain rather than trying to help fix it. I felt so helpless in the face of his condition, and I subconsciously wanted to protect myself from further emotional pain. That morning, I felt emotionally raw and exhausted from the daily stress and worry. I walked in and waited for them to finish cleaning him up and let him rest. He did not wake fully again that day, except to become lucid one more time long enough to say, "Sad."

I looked up at Glenda, who had flown up with only a day's notice when I called to tell her Dean was back in the hospital, and said, "What did he say?"

He mumbled a little more loudly, "Sad."

Again, I looked up in confusion. This time I looked at Karly, who was also hovering over him, and he exclaimed more loudly, "SADNESS!"

We all just froze and looked at each other. Then together, we all teared up realizing what he was saying and continued to help him change his position in the bed.

This haunted me later. What was he trying to say exactly? Did he know at that time he was dying?

Later, the doctor came by and told me that he was no longer responding to the antibiotics. He asked what I would like him to do. At that time, Dean was still on the Dexamethasone and morphine. Since we had intended on bringing him home, I had brought in the marijuana liquid that helped him with pain to get him off the painkiller.

I was in shock. *What?* I screamed in my head. "But he was fine yesterday."

"Unfortunately, he is not getting better. We think the tumor is growing, and he is no longer responding to the antibiotics," the doctor said.

He seemed to recede from my vision, and I felt myself floating outside of my body. I could hear what he was saying, but it wasn't registering.

"But he had an MRI just six weeks ago, and it was stable," I protested. "How could it grow that fast without anyone knowing?"

In that split second, all the control I felt I still had over Dean's illness and care was gone in a nanosecond. I had been buying time, and his time was out. I asked what I should do, and the doctor responded that if we had a DNR in place, maybe we should let nature take its course.

I went silent as I thought about his comments. I told him I needed to think about it and walked away. I hated that from the second Dean had been checked into any hospital since last fall after his stroke, the first thing every doctor wanted to know was where the DNR was and if I had medical authority. I know that they have to do their job, but it was as if they were screaming at me: *We don't believe in you, and your husband is going to die. We don't think you should save him.* In fact, since Dean had the first stroke last October, that was all I heard from any of the doctors—except his current oncologist, who saw the improvement Dean had early into the year and continued to suggest further treatments.

I was not ready for Dean to die, no matter what stage he was at. I had fought and fought and fought, never wanting to give up, and I couldn't slow down. That would mean to lose all hope, which gave me the strength to go on. Without it, the grief became overwhelming.

I was in agony making this decision. "Do I give up? Does he want me to give up?" My situation was so frustrating because Dean never reconciled with dying and never discussed what he wanted me to do if and when things changed.

Do I let him die, or do I continue to do what is necessary to save his life?

He did tell me that he didn't want to be kept alive on a respirator or something of that nature. But the current situation didn't reconcile with needing to be on life support.

In the back of my mind, I knew Dean didn't want to live as he was. Ever since he had the impacted bowels and the headaches had been gaining in strength, he had told me several times that he didn't want to do it anymore. I thought about his pain in the last three days, how he cried out in agony every time they moved him; the suffering in his eyes from the headaches that began every morning when he woke; the emotional pain of being dependent on his wife like an invalid. He was so emasculated. My heart bled for him, and it was excruciating to watch Dean suffer every day.

I went out into the hall so Dean couldn't hear me, even though he was seemingly unconscious. I talked with the on-call doctor at Swedish.

"What can we do for him?" I asked. "He is suffering so horribly."

"If he were my family member, I would increase the pain medication and stop the food and water. I would let him go," he replied.

I listened to this advice and started to tear up. I was screaming in my head, "This is it. This is it."

"I don't want him to suffer anymore," I decided with a heavy heart and painful breath.

I realized my decision was about me not wanting to lose him and not about Dean finding peace from his pain. I agreed to the new plan.

It didn't hit me until later that Tuesday was his last lucid day. I would never get to speak with him again. Later, I would suffer so much grief over missing that time with him.

The situation would go on to change several more times over the next five days, until they finally got the pain medication high enough and the Ativan adjusted to where his body was truly comfortable and stable.

Dean never woke up again. His body went deeper into the coma every day for a total of eight days. Each day, his breathing went through different stages. His body was strong, and he had a strong will to live. It was absolute torture to watch his body die slowly every day for those eight days. That was the most painful thing I have ever gone through in my entire life.

On the night of the twelfth day after admittance, and seven days after being unconscious, Dean waited thirty minutes until we all went home that night to quietly pass away at 8:35 p.m. on March 30, 2016.

We had all been with him night and day, and hospice suggested that we leave him alone. I told him before I left that last night that I would be okay and that it was all right for him to let go. I would still talk to him every day as if he were sitting up and carrying on a conversation with me. But he never actually spoke. I couldn't help thinking back to his last word: Sad ... Sad ... SADNESS! That last night, I cried and begged him to go. It was killing me to watch him die. I needed him to move on. I reminded him that I loved him so much and that he would always be the love of my life.

Even as I left his room, I still expected him to be there in the morning. As I lived through this time in my life, it felt like a movie. I watched events unfold for someone else from a distance and nothing really registered. When they called me at 8:40 p.m. to let me know to come in, I broke down sobbing on the way back to the hospital. I had immediate and all-consuming guilt that I was not with him when he actually took his last breath. We had been together twenty-four hours a day for nine months since his diagnosis, and it still hadn't registered that he would not be with me.

As I walked into that room that I had visited every day for what seemed like an eternity, I looked at my once-beautiful, vibrant husband, who now lay still, broken, and lifeless. All I could focus on was that his face was so white. His mustache was indistinguishable from the color of his skin.

I looked around the room, listening for him. I still expected to see him, even if it was as a ghost.

"Are you here, baby?"

"Where are you?" I spoke into the silence.

"I'm so sorry ... just so sorry ... about everything. That you had to die. That you had so much pain. That you had to leave too soon.

That I couldn't save you. I will miss you until the day I die, when we can be together again," I whispered.

"I will love you for eternity."

I stood there frozen until I realized from the silence that he was truly gone. I walked up to his side and leaned down to kiss his forehead. It was still somewhat warm, which surprised me. That was as close to death as I had ever been. I didn't know what to do. I felt helpless.

Later, when I reflected on that moment, I wished I had lain down next to him for one last time. I would not have had to worry about hurting him, and I could have snuggled up to him and laid my head on his chest. It would have been a temporary stall, but I would have had one more moment to cherish for the rest of my life. But the fact that his body was dead scared me. Death still terrified me.

Finally, I motioned for Lisa and Mike to come in. Glenda and Karly and Matt trailed behind them. They were all out in the hall, waiting to come in. I was a little taken aback, as my sister immediately started sobbing loudly and uncontrollably. She was normally so reserved and strong.

I could not let myself react so viscerally. I held onto my control even though losing my love, my life, was beyond words, and I was in so much pain—emotional and physical pain. Never had life prepared me to watch the man I loved more than anything lie dead in front of me.

PART TWO

AFTERWARD

My story does not end with Dean's death. There was no miracle saving him from his brain tumor. No wonderful story of perseverance or overcoming all odds. He died in nine months. I was never prepared for him to leave; I never gave up hope and continued to fight for his life until the minute he died. I had already been grieving since the day he was diagnosed, and I was still processing my feelings of extreme sadness over the loss of unfulfilled years together and future plans that we had made. Even though he had been very sick and unable to take care of himself, Dean was still my sweet, loving husband, cognitive enough to talk, cry, and laugh with me. Death took him completely away, and until then, I had not fully understood the magnitude of his absence.

As a fifty-two-year-old woman, I had never really been exposed to death. This life-altering experience halted my world. I had to ask myself, "Why doesn't our society teach us about dying?"

When I was around ten years old, I began to have a strong fear of death. It got so bad that I started suffering panic attacks on a regular basis, and my stomach dropped when my mother told me to get ready for bed. I would lie on my back in the dark, my little body ramrod straight, arms tucked in at my hips under the covers that were pulled to my chin, wondering what it would be like if I died. I began to imagine what it would be like to not exist—to be nothing, remember nothing, just as I was before I was born. My heart beat faster and faster, and I found it hard to breathe. I experienced a tingly, terrified feeling in my belly, and my hands and arms felt numb. Sometimes, I got up out of bed to go into my mom's room and tell her my heart hurt. I was distraught that I might be having a heart attack. She would tiredly tell me to go back to bed, and eventually I forced myself to be brave, to shuffle off to my room to go to sleep.

The problem became habitual, so she finally took me to the family physician. He was an older gentleman with gray hair and a kind face, and I wasn't scared of him, which was saying a lot, because I wouldn't even let the dentist look in my mouth. The doctor told her that there was nothing wrong with me and that I was most likely empathizing with her, my mom, because she suffered from frequent debilitating migraines.

I continued to suffer the heart palpitations and abnormal fears for several years. Later, in my twenties, I learned I really did have a heart condition. It was called SVT, Supraventricular Tachycardia, an electrical malfunction to the rhythm of the heart. Maybe my fear of dying aggravated the physical problem, but my first memories were of the anxiety attacks surrounding death.

My fear of death wasn't just at bedtime. I had an abnormal terror of trees falling on our house in windstorms or a tornado coming to wipe out our house. I worried that my parents would forget to pick me up from dance class and that I would somehow perish from being left behind, or that my brother would get separated from us and lost at the mall. I fixated on those apprehensions frequently, along with many other fears all through childhood.

No one wants to talk to children about the concept of death, even though it eventually happens to everyone. Most children are not allowed to go to a funeral. I used to think, "Ohhh, kids don't need to be exposed to such sadness and death."

No one ever taught me how to cope with the death of a family member, and yet it's one of the most shocking and stressful things to happen in one's life. From what I hear, other cultures expose children to the idea of death at an early age; they teach children that it's just part of life. But so many people shelter the young and keep the grief, fear, and anger bottled up inside, pretending on the outside that everything is okay for their own sake. I think it's because as adults, we don't know how to handle it, let alone coach a young person on how to emotionally deal with a loss.

I became obsessed with death after Dean left. I wanted to know if he was okay; I wanted to know where he was. I started to research anything I could find about this online, and I read book after book about the afterlife. I realized how much had already been written about dying and near-death experiences. Anything that I could offer about my story had already been written. But it was new to me. I had never felt anything close to the suffering and grief I was feeling at that point. Learning as much as I could about the afterlife kept me focused on something other than the reality that Dean was gone.

In life, Dean would never accept he was going to die, therefore I could not accept it either. In hindsight, I realize that he was terrified of death, which was one of the reasons why he would not talk about it. For him to check into the hospital with a leg infection, only to die twelve days later, put me into a state of complete shock and denial, even though I knew death from the brain tumor was imminent.

***

The trauma of seeing Dean dead was new to me. I had not seen a dead body before, except for my grandmother, who had already been prepared for burial and was displayed in a casket. Upon his death, all these decisions cropped up immediately. Here I was, still focused on saying goodbye, and the hospital was already asking what funeral home I wanted them to call. I felt relief that Dean was no longer suffering but also guilt and grief for his death. I felt guilty that I did not save his life and that he died without me by his side. How could I cope with all these thoughts and decisions piling up in my head?

I left the hospital for the last time that night. I wouldn't allow my brain to think about anything too deeply. It hurt to breathe in too much air, and I took shallow breaths to compensate. It was as if I was trying to be as still and unmoving as possible so that I could not feel anything emotional or physical. I crawled into bed and looked at my cell phone. It was almost midnight. I had two missed calls. *Who would be calling me at this hour?* I thought.

I listened to a message, and it was a firm that wanted me to approve the donation of Dean's retinas. I called them back right away, and they thanked me profusely for promptly returning their call while confessing their sorrow at my loss.

"Dean's eyes can give two more individuals sight," the woman on the phone said. "Can we have them?"

I thought for a moment.

"Yes. Dean would have wanted that."

In my mind, I was picturing Dean's dead body with no eyes. Another unwanted, gruesome thought I didn't need. I knew it was the right thing to do, though. Even I was an organ donor. Still, it was hard to allow a stranger to touch him, let alone desecrate his body. I felt he and I had lost so much, and I didn't want anyone else taking anything from him at that point. Even though that thought was irrational, as he was being cremated in a couple of days.

They thanked me again, and apologized for bothering me so late.

"We will call you tomorrow for the details so you can get some sleep," the woman said.

I quickly thanked her and hung up. I turned my ringer off so that I would not be disturbed. I really needed a solid eight hours of deep rest. I felt like I hadn't slept in years. I wanted sleep to erase my mind visualizing Dean's body lying alone and cold in the crematorium like a piece of meat. Was his spirit with his body? Was it watching the preparation to remove his eyes? Would he see it burn up? I could not fathom these thoughts, but I couldn't stop worrying about him. I could not shut off what I had been doing nonstop for months.

Four hours later, my phone vibrated. I jumped up in a haze and realized that I had been woken up by the sound of my cell phone. It was still dark out, and I was instantly angry. I knew I had turned all notification sounds off. I leaned over and picked it up to see who was trying to reach me. It was my brother in Washington, DC, sending me a text. I didn't read it but immediately put the phone back down, irritated, and rolled over to go back to sleep.

Suddenly, I heard an owl hooting loudly outside. I slept every night with my bedroom window by the head of my bed cracked open because I would get so hot at night. My body was flooded with a sudden awareness that it was Dean. He was letting me know that he got to heaven and he was okay. I was certain of it. If I had to liken the knowing to something, I would compare it to when you know you are in love. It's intangible but no less real. What is even more strange, I didn't question why I felt it was a sign from him because the knowledge that it was him was so strong.

How many times does anyone hear an owl hoot at four in the morning? That would be the start of many occurrences from Dean to confirm for me that his spirit was still alive with me.

I woke up a couple hours later to the early-morning light filtering through the blinds and could not stop the thoughts racing through my brain. Still numb and running on autopilot, moment to moment, I felt the overwhelming grief crashing into my brain like relentless waves. It slowly penetrated my every waking thought that Dean was dead. I just kept repeating internally in disbelief, *He's gone, really gone.*

This became a pattern. If I was lucky enough to sleep deeply for over four hours, I would wake up feeling, for a brief moment, that everything was normal. Then I would remember that my life was irrevocably changed forever, and all the joy of waking up to a new day deflated like a popped balloon. Then the pain would wash over me. My body would get hot until it reached my face and eyes. The tears would well up and drip down my cheeks like a faucet, and for moments, minutes, or hours, I would lie very still, taking shallow breaths, wanting my life to stop so I could be with Dean.

Glenda was still staying with me the morning after Dean's death, so I got dressed quickly for the day and kept busy, so as not to delve too deeply into my thoughts. We went into a flurry of activity, setting up meetings with the funeral home, calling his mother and brother, and notifying everyone else that Dean was gone. I started working on the video for the memorial, and I had to go pick up flowers and select the music. I had to buy an urn and make all the decisions that come with planning a funeral. I would not let anyone else take care of those decisions. I wanted to do everything. I needed this funeral to honor Dean in the best way I knew how. The activity helped me to mitigate the emotional shock I was in. I could not slow down. Inertia equaled pain.

I began to receive constant advice from different sources—friends, family, counselors, grief groups, clergy, etc.—all of whom gave well-intentioned suggestions about how to deal with my sorrow. There was a similar thread to all of it, and eventually the advice became repetitive. There is no answer to anyone's grief process. Therefore, no one person can help you experience your own loss. Loneliness followed me after the heart-wrenching pain of losing Dean. I felt awkward and unable to fit into social situations.

Comfort came from the "signs" I kept receiving from Dean. A couple of days after the owl incident, Glenda and I were upstairs in the guest bedroom; I lay on the bed while she showed me her dress for the funeral. Suddenly, the lights in only that bedroom went off and on several times, accompanied by a zapping noise. It sounded like something out of *The Twilight Zone*.

"Wow," I said.

Glenda looked around in awe like, "What the …?"

"Hey, baby! Are you hanging out with us, or did you stop in to say hi?" I said, looking up at nothing.

Glenda just laughed, but I knew it was Dean.

THE FUNERAL

The day of Dean's funeral dawned bright and sunny. He would have loved the weather, as he had been a sun worshiper all his life. It was also April 8th, my fifty-third birthday. Dean's mother and brother had flown in from Phoenix, Arizona, the day before, both very emotional and heartbroken. Other than Dean's sister and daughter, no one from the rest of his family had been involved with his illness and death. When they arrived, I found it very difficult to face their emotional reactions as they walked in the door. They both hugged me tight and cried into my shoulder. I fought the urge to pull away, as I found showing my feelings repugnant and withdrew emotionally from their visible grief. I was holding a tight rein on my tears, and I was determined to hold it together until everyone went home.

It was so surreal to me that Dean was gone. How could he be dead when his toothbrush was sitting in the cup next to the bathroom sink? His clothes, wallet, and glasses were scattered throughout the bedroom. The special diet meal delivery food was still in the refrigerator waiting for me to heat and serve. Everywhere I looked in our home—the home we had lovingly built together—reflected his presence. How was I to go on without him? It was starting to sink in that I was really truly alone. I wanted to run away, throw up, or freak out. My skin crawled, and there was an anxiousness that had settled over my head like a cloud. For me, the grief built like a snowball with every day that went by. It would deepen continuously until I felt it was consuming me. At that point in time, I was still experiencing emotional shock. I did not realize how much worse I would feel as time went by.

I leaned heavily on my daughters and Glenda that day. We all headed to the funeral home in different cars: Glenda drove her mom and brother in Dean's truck, the girls drove directly from their homes, and I took my car. It gave me comfort that I would have thirty minutes to myself so that I could release some emotion and cry in private. I chose the funeral home that I had driven by every day when taking Dean to the doctor and going to the hospital. Our company had even striped their parking lot. It was a beautiful old home that looked reminiscent of a southern plantation and reminded me of the funeral home they used in the movie *My Girl*. It was a stately white house with steps leading up to the front door where you entered directly into the grand foyer.

The funeral director was amazing. He took care of the music, videos, and seating. I felt like he was a wedding coordinator and I was the bride with his focus on me and my happiness for the day. The girls and I started making the flower arrangements and setting up the pictures and guest book once we arrived. Tia created the main flower arrangement to set up front on a table, facing the stage. I gently set Dean's urn in the center of the flowers and placed his picture and favorite fishing pole next to it. I had found a bronze fisherman sitting in a rowboat; it was shaped like an oval with an engraved plaque that read, "My handsome husband who always made me laugh, always together forever. If love could have saved you, you would have lived forever." I stepped back and thought how Dean would be so proud of what I had chosen. It was just so him.

People slowly started filing into the room. I felt so awkward and on display. I cowered inside, feeling like everyone was staring at me. I kept wondering what they were thinking: *Why isn't she showing more grief? Shouldn't she act more upset? That poor woman, she is all alone now.*

I was a widow! Wow. I hated that word. I didn't feel or look like a widow; I felt too young to be a widow. When I was married, I marveled at being Mrs. Simmons, excited to have Dean's name and be his bride. Being a widow brought the complete opposite of that euphoria, and I couldn't believe I had to carry that title now.

Karly and Matt came early to help set up the flowers and pictures but brought Dean's ex-wife, Karly's mother, with them. It was one more stressful thing I had to deal with that day. My relationship with her was nonexistent, and Dean's previous interaction with her had been very strained. He had not wanted to see her when he fell ill, and they had not spoken much over the past few years. Personally, I could not stand her, and as they walked in, she approached to give me a very awkward hug. Really? Not once in twelve years had she even acknowledged me or said hello. She smelled of alcohol, and I quickly pulled away.

I brushed the negative feelings off and focused on the unfolding events. Many people came, and it was apparent Dean was very loved. I had chosen the speakers carefully: Mike, my brother-in-law, who had been such a big help through Dean's illness; Chad, my son-in-law, who was filling Dean's shoes in our business; and Jim, Dean's best friend. Jim walked up to the podium first after the director introduced him.

He talked about the years he and Dean had known each other, the trips they'd been on, and how close they were. But most interestingly, he shared that the morning after Dean died, twelve bald eagles flew over his house.

"How odd or rare is it to see twelve bald eagles in one location?" he reflected. "And that they would fly over MY house! Somehow, I knew it was Dean, and he was letting me know he was okay," Jim told everyone.

I thought how symbolic that was for Dean. He'd talked often about how he flew in his dreams almost every night, and it was the superpower he chose when he joked about being a superhero. Lastly, he loved the woods, the outdoors, and animals. He shared those things with Jim, and I thought how amazing it was that Dean chose to give Jim that particular sign.

Mike and Chad went next, and both of them gave the most moving stories as well. I would expand on the beautiful stories they told, but honestly, I can't remember what they said specifically. I just remember that it was perfect and beautiful. None of them could get through the speech without breaking down and crying. It was odd to see these strong grown men cry. I had three videos of Dean, one as a child growing up, then fishing and camping, and finally just the two of us getting married, traveling, and laughing. I played them in between the speeches, and I don't think there was a dry eye in the house.

After the closing remarks, I stood up and walked outside with the family trailing behind me. As we filed out of the row of chairs, it triggered the guests to follow us to the house next door for the buffet of food and drinks. I had no appetite and ended up in a one-person receiving line, hugging and greeting everyone who attended. I heard the following phrases over and over:

"How are you doing?"

"Is there anything I can do to help?"

"You look great!"

How am I supposed to respond to that? I thought. "Ummm, thanks? Death becomes me?"

Nine months later, my mom still asked me every time we spoke, "Are you feeling better?" Like I was recovering from an illness.

Those questions only brought awareness to the emotional gap and isolation I felt when greeting someone, which only made me want to run and hide even more.

Eventually, I was able to break free and go sit with my best friend, Brenda. I marveled at how many people enjoyed staying and reminiscing about Dean, so much so that the funeral home ran out of food. The warm summer-like evening was ideal, and no one was in a hurry to leave. Finally, after four hours, almost everyone had gone, and I felt like I could get away. I carefully gathered Dean's picture and urn and slipped out. As I drove home, I felt a wonderful sense of accomplishment that Dean was honored in a beautiful way and that he would have been so happy. I had a deep knowing that he had attended his own funeral and was joyful of such a wonderful celebration of his life.

SIGNS

Dean's family had finally gone home, and it was my first night alone. It had been eleven days since his death. I could finally breathe. I had been holding in my grief and emotions, and now they erupted out of me in a hail of salty tears, snot, and loud sobbing. I looked around me. It was so surreal that all of Dean's things were now mine. The house, the business, and all the stuff comprising his life was only mine. He had at least thirty fishing poles, top-of-the-line hunting gear, and tools in the garage.

What am I supposed to do with everything? I can't possibly give his stuff away, I told myself. It didn't seem right.

I could not disturb any of his things. Being alone now, after being with Dean every minute of every day for the last nine months, seemed wrong. My world was messed up. I felt lost without him.

What am I supposed to do with myself now?

I was surprisingly not scared to be home alone at night. Years before, after we had first built our house, Dean used to stay out of town for work. I would be terrified by myself, so I set up night-lights all over the house. We lived in a remote location on ten acres, and I could not see my hand in front of my face when the power went out. I would leave all the lights on in the house when I had to go to bed and complain to Dean that I never got any rest without him by my side.

I think on some level, I felt Dean's presence with me since he passed and had not been scared to sleep alone since his death.

On that first night, after all the company was gone, something woke me up at 12:20 a.m. I sensed movement, as if someone was in the room. I came fully awake and sat up, staying very still to listen. It sounded like furniture was being moved upstairs, and I could hear muffled thumping. I couldn't believe I was nervous and thought, here I go, already frightened to sleep alone in my own house. I jumped out of bed and walked out into the living room and listened intently. I heard nothing. Perplexed, I came back into the bedroom and laid back down. I tried to go back to sleep, but the sound was still there. I tried to ignore it, but I couldn't stop my ears from straining to figure out what the noise was. With much annoyance, I stood up again. I walked toward the dresser, where the flat-screen TV hung above, and all the stereo components sat inside. I put my ear to the wall, and I could feel and hear the vibrations. I realized that the sounds were coming from the TV cable box.

"Urghhh," I growled. I was so mad.

I found sleep so elusive, and lack of rest was just one more problem contributing to my daily fatigue. I bent down and ripped the surge protector out of the wall. All the components went black, and I heard the sound of all the electronics powering off. I climbed back into bed, determined to get some rest.

No sooner had I lain back down than the entire dresser with all the electronic components inside it started to vibrate as if there were an earthquake. My heart jumped, and the sound of it pounded in my ears. I sat up, feeling nervous. I didn't understand what was happening, as I had never experienced anything like it.

I tentatively said, "Dean is that you? Are you okay?" I anxiously waited, but there was no answer.

"I love you. I miss you." I held my breath, and my eyes teared up. I yearned to hear his voice or see some sign of his existence, even though in my heart I knew he was gone. Still, there was something happening, and I wanted to know what it was.

I stood up for a third time and walked toward the dresser when suddenly, the dresser and TV components started to vibrate violently for a second time. I jumped back, startled by the movement. I knew there was no way anything could be causing the surge of electricity, as none of the components were plugged in anymore. I sat on the edge of the bed. I wasn't sure what to do, and my heart continued to pound with excitement and a little fear. I realized that this time there was no mistaking something was happening beyond my comprehension.

"Dean, is that you?" I repeated. "Do you need something? Where are you?" I half whispered.

There was only silence, but I felt an energy in the room that I had never felt before. I felt my body rejecting the energy sensations out of fear yet also opening up to the possibility that Dean could really be with me. I was so overwhelmed with emotion that I didn't know what to do, so I hesitantly climbed back into bed and lay down. I listened intently for a while until I finally, out of exhaustion, fell back asleep. I awoke again at 2:00 a.m. to a loud noise sounding like something fell behind the dresser. I sensed a presence, and I groggily looked up and around but did not see anyone or anything that could have fallen to make a loud noise. I realized there was nothing to threaten or hurt me, so I lay back down to sleep once again. It was amazing how quickly my mind had adjusted to the thought of a spirit or ghost trying to communicate with me. But the thought that it was Dean took away any fear of the unknown.

Within two hours, while I lay sleeping, a bright flash went off in my face, startling me awake. My eyes flew open again, and I realized it was still dark outside. I looked at the clock, and it was only 4:00 a.m. Dean was definitely trying to get my attention. It was like someone had taken my picture with a flashbulb right in front of me. I didn't know what to make of this phenomenon. I had never thought about spirits in this way. I don't know how I knew this was Dean—I just did.

I had heard similar stories of spiritual events, but never really put a lot of thought into actually living them myself. I realize it's really hard to explain without seeming crazy. There was never a question in my mind that these events were happening from Dean's spirit. What was even more surprising was that I had no fear from anything that was taking place. I only felt excitement and curiosity. Could this be Dean trying to communicate with me? Nothing could have made me happier. All I knew was that I wanted more signs to confirm that what I felt was real.

The next morning, I looked behind the dresser to see what had fallen, and there was nothing there but the cord of the surge protector lying on the carpet—the surge protector I had already ripped out of the wall hours earlier. As I absorbed the nightly events that had happened, I became further determined to learn about life after death.

LIFE MOVES ON WITH OR WITHOUT ME

While Dean was dying, and then after he passed away, our business continued moving forward. I had delegated 95 percent of my work to Hannah, Tia, Chad, and Enrique so I could focus on being with Dean. During that time, I made one of the biggest financial mistakes in the history of starting our company. The crew needed another work vehicle, so I drove to look at a used truck a couple days after Dean's death and took one of my foremen with me. I had him test-drive an F-450 Flatbed, and since it appeared fine, I bought it for $32,000 within a thirty-minute time frame. The truck engine blew up three weeks later. Being that it had a diesel engine, it was going to cost $18,000 to repair. My loan on the balance of the truck was more than that, so I could not refinance it. I was devastated. This was a huge financial hardship, and I felt stupid for not investing more time into researching this purchase. The engine had only sixty thousand miles, so it was unheard of for this type of engine to fail, or so I thought.

Other business problems cropped up daily during that time to compound my anxiety and stress. We had several jobs that lost money, and I would later find out they were underbid or we had major labor inefficiencies. Those were jobs that Dean had taken care of in the past. I felt lost without his expertise and judgment on all fieldwork.

Also during that time, my short-term memory became terrible and continued to get worse over the next year. I stopped remembering appointments, people's names, and jobs I had scheduled. I would excuse my behavior, saying I had "grief" brain, but I was secretly horrified that I could not follow through the way I would have in the past.

One day, I was getting a coat out of the hall closet. All of Dean's coats were still hanging next to mine, so I grabbed one of his and started to sniff it. I could not smell his scent, so I frantically ripped every one of his coats out of the closet then started on his shirts in our bedroom, throwing everything on the floor as I went. I must have looked like a crazy person. I smelled the collars, armpits, and sleeves, desperate for a wisp of him. Dean did not wear cologne, and he always smelled like fresh, clean skin. I was OCD when it came to laundry and cleaning, and I could not find a shirt he'd worn and hung up that hadn't already been washed. I collapsed in a heap on the stairs in the hallway, almost hyperventilating, tears streaming down my face.

"I can't smell you. I can't smell you!" I screamed to the ceiling.

But the only response was silence. I fell on the stairs out in the hallway and cried until I was out of tears. Later, I finally picked myself off the floor and continued on with my day, my face swollen and head pounding. I would have many episodes like that over the next few months.

Why didn't I take videos of him before he was really sick? Why didn't I think to save his voice messages on my phone? When his daughter and brother forwarded me some of their recordings off their phones, I cried so hard when I heard his voice, I thought I popped blood vessels in my face. I never thought he would die, so I never thought to take videos of him or save voice recordings. That was one of my biggest regrets.

As I found Dean's things scattered about the house, like his daily calendar for work, I would read them for any details about his thoughts or appointments. I read and reread the texts we sent to each other, starting before his diagnosis and going up until right before he died, tearing up every time. One text was when we were together and he was waiting for me at the hair salon, he had texted "You have a cute butt."

I laughed as I looked across the room at him, and he gave me that secret smile to say *I knew I could make you laugh.* He had sent me random texts saying, "I love you" or his happy messages that he was on his way home to have dinner with me. I was always excited to see his phone calls or texts on my cell phone, and my heart would flutter just like it did when we first started dating, even after twelve years of being together. As I came across every note he wrote or text he sent me, my heart would break all over again.

I desperately needed a connection to him, and I wore his clothes every night. As soon as I got home from running errands or returning from work, I would put on one of his T-shirts, flannel pajama bottoms, and socks, wearing them until the next morning. I even wore his underwear. When he was first diagnosed, I bought him a gold chain with a cross on it and told him it was to have faith. I wear that same necklace now, only I added his wedding ring to it. And after he died, I purchased a pendant with his thumbprint on it. It's shaped into a heart, and I put it on a necklace with a cross he had given me as a gift for my birthday. Sometimes, when the pain of missing him overtakes me, I grip the necklace tight in my fist, valiantly channeling his spirit to comfort me.

I became somewhat antisocial during this time. Well-meaning friends and family would text or call to check up on me. I would respond that I was doing fine. I could not explain how I felt, as it was just too personal, and I only wanted to be left alone. Slowly, over the next couple of months, they all stopped reaching out.

I was okay with that because it was exhausting pretending to be fine. I hated answering questions every time I saw someone. It was a lie, and I'm not good at lying. Eventually, as I started to receive more signs from Dean, I didn't want to go anywhere. I wanted to connect with him in any way I could. So, I stayed at home in my room and waited for anything that would connect me with him.

Unfortunately, there was no predictability to when or how his spirit would reach out to me, so I spent many days and nights alone in my room, just waiting and hoping he would show up.

DAD

"Hello?" I answered my cell phone one morning, nine days after Dean's funeral.

"Nitch?" my sister said.

"Yeah? What's up?" I asked.

"Mom found Dad on the floor beside the bed this morning. He got up to go to the bathroom sometime in the middle of the night and collapsed. He was barely lucid and couldn't communicate, so she called 911. She said his right side isn't moving, and the only way he could convey his feelings was through his eyes. They took him to Swedish Urgent Care," she hurriedly rattled off the details to me.

"Can you come and meet Mike and me at the hospital?"

"I'm on my way!" I shouted as I looked around the house for my purse. It was a sad fact that I could fall right back into panic mode and calmly absorb crisis at a moment's notice.

I immediately jumped in the truck to drive to meet everyone at the hospital. Of course, it was the same hospital Dean had just died in. As my mind reeled with concern and disbelief over what was seemingly happening again, only this time to my dad, I suddenly felt overwhelmed. I burst into tears, blinding me as I drove. Suddenly, the words to a song playing on the radio penetrated my brain. I heard the chorus to a song by Rachel Platten called "Stand By You." As the words sunk in, I was comforted with the knowledge that Dean was there with me and speaking to me through a song. I felt Dean's presence sitting next to me, and I was calmed.

It was another beautiful day in Seattle, but I barely noticed the sunshine. It seemed the weather was always the direct opposite of the drama in my life. I raced to the hospital, parked, and ran inside. Dad was in the emergency room, lying on the gurney. I rushed up to his bedside, brushing past my sister, mom, and brother-in-law. He looked at me worried, trying to speak through the emotion conveyed through his eyes.

"Dad, are you all right?" I asked. "I'm sure you're going to be fine. Hang in there until we find out what's going on, okay?"

He flailed his left arm and hand. I handed him a piece of paper and a pen to see if he could communicate by writing, but he just looked at me, not knowing what to do.

How awful that he was trapped in his body with no way to communicate his needs or what happened to him. I tried asking him some questions to see if he could blink for yes or no, but he didn't comprehend even that simple task.

I felt myself mentally sliding back into that dark place—the place of fear, anxiety, and stress—as I sat in the same room Dean had been in barely one month earlier when he suffered from the horrible headaches after we reduced his Dexamethasone.

"Where are the doctors?" I asked my sister.

"We are waiting for them to come and take him for a CT scan. They think he had a stroke. That's why he can't speak or move his right side."

"Wow. I can't believe this is happening. And so soon after Dean," I said.

I still naively thought Dad was going to be okay. We sat and waited until the CT tech came by to take Dad away. Mom was an emotional mess. She was crying and fluttering around like a bird.

"Mom, why don't you go and get something to eat?" I asked her.

"I'm not hungry, I just can't eat anything right now," she said.

But her muttering, crying, and inability to sit still were stressing me out. My mom was not a positive person, and as we continued to wait, she became more morose and negative, which did not help the situation.

Dad wasn't gone long and was soon wheeled back into the room with us. It was Mike, Lisa, Mom, and me this time, waiting on the test results so that we knew what had happened to Dad. Over an hour later, after they had completed the blood work and CT scan, I started wandering out into the hall and staring at the nurses and doctor to see if they would hurry up. I could see them studying the negatives of the CT scan but could not figure out why they were delaying in telling us what they discovered. In the meantime, Dad would flail his left arm and act like he wanted to sit up over and over. We had to constantly calm him down and keep him in the bed so he would not hurt himself.

Finally, the on-call urgent care doctor came in to give us the results. The whole routine felt like déjà vu to me. This time, unlike with Dean, he called us out of the room to tell us the results of the CT scan.

"I'm sorry it took so long for the results," he said.

"We wanted to get a second opinion from the neurologist in our downtown hospital. I'm really sorry, but the stroke your dad suffered was massive. It wiped out most of the cognitive function of his right side. Even if we were to treat him, the swelling would continue to worsen. That would cause further decline, and there is no rehabilitation or recovery of his brain. After three months, he might be back to where he is now, bedridden for the rest of his life. He cannot eat on his own, swallow, talk, walk, or have the use of his right side again. His quality of life would be as it is at this moment."

Lisa, Mike, and I just looked at each other. Mom was not the executor on Dad's health care directive—Lisa was. Mom and Dad were legally separated, so Lisa had power of attorney on whether to try and continue Dad's life or end it. I felt horrible that she had to make the same decision I had to make four weeks ago for Dean.

It's sad how life changes so quickly after sailing along for years with the mild ups and downs. Here we were, in our early fifties, facing life-and-death decisions for not one but two people we loved. Oddly enough, Lisa told me that the day of Dean's funeral, Dad had come to her house looking for his will and health care directive. He told her that he knew he was next. He saw what brain cancer had done to Dean. He told her that he did not want to live like that and that if he were to get sick, he did not want her to prolong his life.

What! I now said to myself. *It is so weird that he knew that. How did he know that? Is there some internal voice that alerts us about when we are going to die?*

We all stood there, lost in our own thoughts but facing each other like we were in a conversation. We were stalling; we all knew what needed to be done, but we were prolonging the decision that would make it reality. Concurrently, the doctor was making arrangements for Dad to be transferred to a room upstairs. We reentered the room and sat down. No one said much, but we all knew that Dad's life was over. Mom started to cry once Lisa explained what needed to happen, and suddenly, I couldn't breathe.

"The waiting is intolerable. I have to go," I told everyone. "I can't do this. It's too soon after Dean's death, and I feel like I'm suffocating here in this hospital."

Everyone fully understood and urged me to go home. I left the building feeling so guilty. Here I was again, leaving the hospital when I should be staying there to help and be supportive. I hated myself for being such a coward.

The next day, I drove back to the hospital to sit and wait with everyone in the room Dad was given. Of course, it was on the same floor Dean had been on and in the same wing, which just reminded me more of losing him. Lisa was battling the insurance and hospice for medical coverage so that Dad could stay. Dad was in his own room but technically should have gone home on hospice, as there was no way doctors were actively trying to save his life. The goal was to make him comfortable, but the doctors pulled him off food and water so as not to prolong his life. They told us that when the brain suffers such a trauma, the patient doesn't feel hungry or thirsty anymore. Lisa knew that Mom could not care for Dad twenty-four hours a day by herself. At least at the hospital he had a whole team of nurses and doctors helping to attend to his every need.

The doctors were also aware that we had all just been there for two weeks while Dean died, and so they went the extra mile to make things work. I felt that the doctors and nurses at Swedish were amazing. They were kind and helpful when our world was falling apart. It takes special people to be so caring with families who are already overwrought that their loved ones are dying, then help them through those deaths.

As I walked into Dad's room that morning and saw him lying in the bed, I was determined to be positive and cheerful for him. I sat down on the edge of the bed and looked into his eyes and said, "Hi, Dad. I love you."

He kind of half smiled, and I knew that he understood me. I didn't know what else to say since he could not respond, or maybe I offered words of comfort, but I don't remember. Eventually, I walked over and sat down by the window. The staff had brought the fruit and cookie platter in for us, which I felt was so thoughtful.

I kept having feelings of déjà vu since I had just done this for two weeks with Dean. Suddenly, I started to feel claustrophobic again. My mother kept muttering about my Dad's hair, saying it was smelly and dirty and needed to be washed. She wouldn't sit still and kept cleaning up anything in the room she could find. Her need to constantly be moving or complaining was grating on my nerves.

She turned to me and tearfully said, "Now I know what you went through with Dean. Oh, but you were only together for twelve years, not like Al and I were together for forty plus years."

I was offended at that statement. It felt like she was comparing my love for Dean with hers for Dad, and that my grief could not possibly be as bad as hers since their union had been longer. They had been separated for fifteen years and had a complicated, rocky marriage for much longer. And anyway, who says something like that? I ignored her statement and didn't respond.

Later, Tia and Hannah came by to say goodbye to their grandpa. As they stood there, Mom asked them if they wanted some of Dad's things. I was appalled at this blatantly insensitive behavior. After the girls left, I confronted her. "Mom, it's not right that you are giving Dad's things away when he can hear you and hasn't even died."

"Oh, that's ridiculous," she said. "He can't hear me!" She huffed.

"Yes, he can. And I find it hurtful that you are acting this way. You have already gone home and started cleaning out his room and giving away his things. Why would you do that when he hasn't even departed yet?"

"He doesn't care. I can't say anything right around you!" she exclaimed.

I stopped talking, knowing there was no reasoning with her. By then my sister had returned from the café.

"I need to go," I told her. "I can't stay here. This is just too much for me to handle. Is it all right? Will you be okay without me?" I asked her.

"Yes, I will be fine. Mike is coming back, and Mom is here. I will keep you posted," she assured me.

Again, I left feeling guilty that I was not staying to help my sister. But watching Dad slowly die and listening to my mom was more than I could take.

My feelings were so complicated during that time. My dad and I had never had a close relationship. He had been an alcoholic since he was twelve years old and was never emotionally available to me. I loved my Dad, but I never really felt close to him.

I never had a strong connection with him as a father figure. I loved him as my father, but I remember as a child watching movies where a father would offer advice to his daughter about life, love, or dreams, and I didn't understand the connection or support shown to her. The saying was true that I didn't miss what I didn't know.

Now he was dying, and I would never really know who he was. It made me sad, and it made me mad. Why didn't I get that kind of love from him? But I bottled up all those feelings and shut down emotionally through his death. All I had to give was eaten up with grief for my husband, who had loved me so much. He was what was important, I told myself. I couldn't absorb more pain than I already had.

I went back to visit Dad one more time before his death in the next five days. My brother, Tony, who was in the middle of a climb at Mount Everest, had to take a helicopter off the mountain and travel three days to get back to Seattle, so that he could say goodbye to Dad. The hospital helped to keep Dad lucid for my brother by giving him an IV of fluids for an extra day. Tony wanted to talk to Dad and frantically traveled through storms and airline delays starting from Kathmandu to get back as quickly as possible. He arrived just in time because after that day, Dad fell into a coma.

He died the morning of the fifth day, quickly and quietly. Lisa and Tony were with him, but as he took his last breath, my sister was on the phone with my mom, who was upset because of something Lisa had said to her. Lisa cried out that she thought he had just died, but Mom had already hung up on her. Lisa tried calling her back so she would know Dad was gone, but my mother wouldn't answer the phone. Finally, my brother had to drive to her house and personally tell her to come back to the hospital. My sister was very upset with her after that. She felt the unnecessary drama took something away from Dad transitioning. Ultimately, it was my sister and brother who were there for my dad when he took his last breath. I was glad he was not alone.

Lisa was wonderful and handled the funeral through the same mortuary that I used for Dean. They were concerned but caring that we were back so soon. My mother did not want to have a funeral for my dad, saying it wasn't necessary, but Lisa knew that Dad would have wanted it at the Catholic church. He had been a regular patron for years and had gone every Sunday ever since I could remember. Lisa contacted the priest at the church my dad had attended so faithfully and set up the ceremony for him. She decided to have him cremated, as that was his wish, and set the memorial for May 6th.

It felt odd that I wasn't more involved with the event. I felt as if there was a wall up in my brain that was blocking all emotions regarding my dad. Regardless, Memorial Day—Friday, May 6th— dawned bright and sunny. Once again, the weather was in direct contrast to my life. I dressed in black and drove to the Catholic church located on the Sammamish Plateau. It was a typical Catholic church, an understated modern building with a lot of brick.

I walked into the main entry and immediately saw the picture boards of Dad's life and fresh flower arrangements surrounding the closed oak double doors that led into the sanctuary. I still wasn't used to attending events without Dean, and I kept reminding myself that I was alone now. I took a deep breath and approached the funeral director, who had handled Dean's memorial.

"Good morning! How are you?" I asked.

"I'm doing well. More importantly, how are you doing?" he asked.

"I'm okay," was my stock answer.

How did I say that I was completely heartbroken my husband was gone and now my dad was dead?

Uncles, aunts, cousins, and friends slowly filtered into the waiting area. Lisa had set up a nice video montage of different pictures of Dad over the years. I meandered over to watch it until they opened the big double doors. The waiting area was huge, and it made the number of people attending seem small.

145

I had never experienced a Catholic funeral before. There were a couple of singers, and then the priest came out and said some prayers. He talked about Dad for a while and then did this weird ceremony over his urn with smoke that smelled of some kind of incense. It was really quite beautiful, and when they sang "Ave Maria" I teared up, as I knew Dad would have loved it.

When it was over, the priest handed each of my family members a part of the ceremonial items. Mom carried the urn, I carried a picture, and Lisa and Tony carried the other items that had been up front. Then we all filed out to the waiting area and kept walking to the front curved driveway until we were standing behind a black hearse. Then the items were taken from us one by one and set into the back of the car. As the hearse drove off (more for ceremony, than for practicality), I sobbed loudly, which took me by surprise. I hated showing public emotion, and I knew everyone there was looking at me with sorrow and pity. The sadness I felt overwhelmed me. I could not contain my anguish at the realization that, not only was my husband dead, but my dad was dead too—and in a span of less than four weeks. I felt abandoned, scared, and so very sad.

I brushed off the attention and left to the restroom to collect myself. When I came back out, everyone had moved into a big open room with nicely decorated white linen tables. Along the wall was a huge spread of food, all homemade and contributed to the event from the local parishioners. Karly sat with me and kept me company, and I relaxed with the normal chatter going on around the table.

Suddenly, my brother got up and walked to a pulpit and started to tell a story about Dad. It was funny and poignant, and I loved that he could reminisce about him that way. This started a train of others to come up and share their stories, and many of my uncles who spoke told stories I had never heard before. The funeral ended on such a sweet note, and I felt warmed that I was a part of such a close and loving family. My dad would have been proud of this remembrance, and I hoped he had been there in spirit. I left the funeral feeling emotionally and physically exhausted.

As I walked to my car, all I wanted to do was go home and crawl in bed. I longed for some kind of magic to knock me out so I did not have to feel the emotional and physical pain. I felt so lonely and lost. Life was making up for lost time. I hadn't realized how easy I had it until now.

SPIRIT

As time went on, I continued to have many signs that Dean's spirit was not only alive but also with me as well. It started with his strong sense of presence in the car or truck everywhere I went. I found myself laying my right hand out to hold his hand while I drove, just like I did when he was alive. I would do this subconsciously and catch my hand reaching out for his. I had repeated nightly activity that always seemed to be around 2:00 a.m. when my bedroom TV components all started to click off. The proof for me was that the power only went off to everything plugged into a surge protector with no other outages to anything else in the house. This seemed to be a prominent way Dean would show me he was around; I just didn't know what he was trying to tell me.

My next impactful experience was on April 12th, thirteen days after Dean died. I was in that in-between state of being awake and asleep. I felt movement on Dean's side of the bed; it felt so natural, as

I was used to him sleeping next to me, that it did not surprise me. I felt him roll over and engulf me in a hug, and I had this indescribable euphoric feeling. I was so happy and felt an incredible saturation of love infused into my body. As I moved to hug him back, overjoyed he was with me, I woke up fully. Then I realized he was gone, and the loss of those feelings was like falling into a black abyss taking me back to despair and depression.

I knew that I had not imagined all the signs or the dream that felt so real. I decided I wanted to learn more about what was happening to me and thought about seeking out a medium. Later that day, I went on the Internet to research and read about the available mediums in my area. I wanted someone to come to me, and I was worried about picking the wrong person and getting scammed. I had always had an open mind about mediums and spirits but never put a lot of thought into it, as I had never lost anyone really close to me. I knew that it was critical that I find just the right person, just as I knew there were a lot of frauds. After reading about several different people, I settled on a medium named Lisa. She was in the Seattle area and had many good reviews. She advertised about helping to heal from a loved one's loss. I realized how many others seek out mediums when losing someone close. I was not doing anything that was unique by any means. According to the American Federation of Certified Psychics and Mediums, 69 percent of women and 39 percent of men have admitted to consulting with a medium. These figures astounded me at first, but after much thought, I realized that this was the first time I felt I needed to reach out to someone in the afterlife. If it was so easy for me to believe, why not others?

I want to say that I am relaying my experiences only. I cannot speak for anyone else's beliefs or values. I was working off my intuition, and it was strongly telling me that Dean was still alive but in a different way. I only wanted to connect to him to find out if he was okay and tell him I loved him. I had no other motivation, and in my quest for more information, I found many others with similar experiences. There was a strong thread amongst grief-stricken people like me, open to what is not tangible, willing to experience and learn more than the eye can see. If not for the experience or knowledge, then to connect to the ones loved and lost.

I was disappointed that most of the mediums I found would not meet with a client until three months had passed after death. I guess it was something about letting a spirit get settled into a new environment and being able to become strong enough to connect to the one reaching out. I booked my appointment with Lisa in late July. It seemed like such a long wait to me, as every day—sometimes every breath—was an effort to get through. But just having a scheduled date gave me hope and made me happier. It was not like he was going anywhere anyway.

In the meantime, a few days later, I received an email from my sister. She had a woman that she worked with who mentioned she had lost her husband three years ago and had heard about my loss. She conveyed her sorrow over Dean's death and wanted to know if I was interested in seeing a clairvoyant to help me with my grief. Lisa instantly told her that she and I had just been talking about that very subject and that I would be very interested. So, the woman emailed my sister, enclosing the intuitive's name and phone number, and mentioned that her experience had been very healing and positive, so much so that three years later, she was remarried and happy again.

As soon as I received the referral, I called her that minute. The woman's name was En-May, and she answered her phone on the second ring. I thought that was amazing, as none of the other mediums had been available by phone. I tentatively told her my name and how I had found her, asking if she could help me. She was very sweet and kind and assured me that she most definitely could help me out. Even more exciting, she was willing to see me right away. We quickly set an appointment for three weeks out.

I was getting ready to go on a trip to Europe with my sister and brother-in-law and would meet with her as soon as I got back. Later she told me that Dean had brought me to her. I was extremely excited and couldn't wait to meet with her. How fortuitous that I had found her so quickly when I felt I needed some relief from the many questions and feelings overwhelming me. Now I just had to get through the trip to Europe.

EUROPE

While my sister sat with me in the hospital in the last two weeks of Dean's life, she surprised me with an invitation to go on a European cruise with her and Mike. At the time, I thought, wow, that would be an escape and a chance for me to get away from the horror of the last nine months. I would be able to see Europe, something I had always wanted to do, and distract myself from the grief of losing my husband. I don't think it was such a good time to be making decisions, but I happily agreed—anything to take my mind off my life that was spinning out of control.

Almost two months after Dean passed, I semi-excitedly packed my bags, got my passport in order, and hired a house sitter to take care of Cady, my dog. I felt emotionally stable about embarking on the trip until we loaded onto the airplane. As soon as I took my seat, I realized I was next to a vacant chair and that it might not have been such a good idea to travel without Dean. I immediately felt heartbroken that I was on a plane without him sitting next to me. I missed his presence, the feel of his hand on my lap, and the comfort that he gave me in case of a crash, that we would still be together. I tried very hard to keep it together, as I didn't want to cry in front of the strangers boarding the plane. I felt so isolated and vulnerable and didn't want anyone to see me upset. Yet, here I was going on a two-week vacation, feeling lonelier than ever.

I turned my head into the row of four seats to hide my face. There was a man sitting in the fourth seat down from mine, leaving two vacant seats in-between. He was heavy, and I watched him absently as he took off his shoes and socks. Suddenly, my mind was taken from my pain to absorb the reality that this fat, sweaty man sitting in my row had his disgusting bare feet exposed for the ten-hour flight to London. If it wasn't so crazy, I would have laughed out loud.

Once we arrived at the docks in London, we loaded on the cruise liner. It was the same boat Dean and I had traveled on to the Caribbean two years previously; it was named *The Ruby*. Everywhere I looked I had memories of the fun we'd shared. It emphasized the fact that once more, I was alone, and it only compounded my isolation.

While on this trip, I suffered horrible insomnia. I was lucky to get three to four hours of sleep a night. I spent many hours alone in my little ship room watching the TV they gave me or reading books I checked out of the ship library. My room was hot, and I was restless; I would do anything to take my mind off my grief. I rose at 4:30 a.m. and walked the deck that circled the entire ship to help release my anxiety and tire me out. I found comfort in my room because I could cry and release my emotions in private, but after hours of being cooped up, I felt suffocated.

I found myself walking laps around the ship several times a day; it invigorated me. The wind, sun, and sea were all that Dean loved. My emotions would rebound from one extreme to another. I would feel euphoric as I walked, breathing in the fresh sea air and soaking in the weak sun, but then on the next thought, I would despair because I missed Dean so badly. Sometimes, my whole body would ache for him. I felt I was trying to reach him mentally and, on some level, physically at all times I was alone. During our marriage, I avoided doing anything without him—like taking a vacation or trip—I couldn't enjoy it because new experiences were not fun without Dean to share it with. To experience the European seas alone was just so sad.

In addition to arriving in London, our cruise boat docked at various ports in Scotland, Ireland, and France. The weather was very cold and some days pouring down rain. I did not realize that these countries were farther north of the equator than Seattle. I didn't know if the weather was matching my mood, but I felt it was very gloomy in most ports and didn't see the beautiful sunny green rolling fields with fluffy white sheep as I had seen on TV or in the movies.

Our first stop was in a little town called Guernsey. Lisa and Mike were not going to go into port, but I was anxious to get off the ship. I decided to go alone and headed down to the exit off the boat, but when I got to the tenders, they were rocking so hard from the waves I worried I would get seasick. I boarded one of them and tentatively sat on one of the hard interior benches for a few minutes. I immediately felt seasick, and I looked around nervously, wondering how long it would be before the boat moved. The crew was waiting for the boat to fill up, and soon I decided to get off and wait on the little dock beside the tender until it was ready to leave. Once it started to move I knew I would not get seasick.

Finally, it was time to go, so I jumped off the dock back onto the tender and climbed up to the top level out in the light rain and wind so that I could keep the breeze in my face. It quickly became very cold, and I huddled into my raincoat for warmth. I felt lonely, so I made some photography small talk with a couple of other passengers next to me who had big cameras like mine.

Once we docked, I took off at a brisk walk into town. I was excited to finally be at our first destination and looked around in wonder at this small seaside town. It looked like a postcard with quaint buildings painted in bright yellows, oranges, and blues. The clay roofs gave the buildings an old-world charm, and I had to remind myself that I was really in Europe. Everyone scattered as they took off for their own destinations, but I kept walking directly into town until the road ended at a small windy cobblestone path. The town seemed to be deserted, and I wondered if it was too early in the morning for Europeans to be up. I read somewhere that I should do something that scares me every day, so I slowly walked up the road that snaked between the old shops until pretty soon I realized I was the only one around. All the stores were empty of people, and the road was empty of cars and bikes.

Suddenly, I heard footsteps coming my way. I turned and saw a man in a black trench coat and hat walking toward me. My steps faltered, and I hesitated to keep walking ahead. I kept my head down, and out of the corner of my eye I watched his moves carefully in case he walked across the street toward me. Luckily, he kept moving, and I hurried past him until I came to the end of the street.

That was too much risk for me, so I found a road that wound back down toward the dock where all the tourists were. I noticed that some of the locals had Mohawks and pink hair, lots of body piercings, and tattoos. It kind of reminded me of the characters in the movie *The Kingsman*. I could hear the strong accents as they talked, and I found it fascinating. I walked safely around an old castle that was right on the water next to the docks. I took lots of pictures and then headed back to the next boat tender to take me to the ship.

Later I emailed my daughter, Tia, about my experience, and she wrote back, "Mom, maybe you don't need to wander around alone in a strange town to do something that scares you. Stick with something like dancing or a new hobby."

I had to laugh.

We went on to stop at ports in Dublin, Blarney, and Belfast in Ireland; Glasgow and Invergordon, Scotland; Versailles in France; and one of my favorites, Liverpool, England. I found the different cities beautiful but felt that a lot of the landscape reminded me of Seattle. Whether it was Eastern Washington or west of the mountains, the green foliage, rolling hills, and rain felt like home. If not for the different clay roofs and style of housing, I could have been in the Northwest.

It's amazing to me that even though I was on a different continent, there was such a commonality amongst all people and places everywhere. The locals rush around, cell phones in hand, living life just like people at home, only in a different part of the world.

Even though it was a wonderful experience, wherever I went and whatever I saw, I never stopped thinking about or missing Dean. I knew there was a life lesson somewhere in Dean's death—I just couldn't figure out what it was yet. Going on this trip, I felt like half of me was missing, so I could not enjoy it to the fullest. I realized I could not run away from the pain.

MEDIUMS

As soon as I got back from the cruise, I excitedly looked forward to my first medium reading. With much anticipation, I arrived at En-May's office, which was a small room in a large older office complex. I was early, so I sat down in a chair right outside the office door to wait for her to show up. Not too much later, a small Japanese woman with a sparkle in her eyes and a kind, quiet voice walked up and smiled at me. I jumped up and confirmed who I was and gave her a hug. That was unlike me, as I'm not a touchy-feely kind of person. I don't know why, but I felt like I already knew her and felt comfortable in her presence right away.

I sat down on the edge of a comfortable love seat, and she sat down in a chair next to me. I looked around the room that was small but cozy; it felt almost like a sitting room at home rather than an office. There was a coffee table in front of us, and I set my phone down. I then promptly forgot to record the session, as I was just too excited and nervous. No sooner had we gotten comfortable than she immediately told me that she had meditated on me earlier that morning. She shared that she saw me as a small girl that never got the love she needed as a child. I had a learned behavior that I could not feel safe or loved unless I had a man in my life to give me that.

"What?" I thought for a moment. I just met this person, and she nailed a personal deep behavior I had been carrying around for years and didn't realize until just that moment. *This experience is going to be interesting*, I thought. She went on to say that I would fall deeply in love again, in around three years and would remarry. I exclaimed that I would never get married again, and she quickly responded, "Whatever."

I learned as time went on that she never argued with me but only stated the facts of what she envisioned and what her intuition told her. Since her revelations were the future, it was hard to reconcile with current feelings and knowledge. Her visions were also not linear in time. When I questioned her about an event, she would respond with what she saw, but it was not necessary to the time period of what I was focused on.

She started off right away with, "Your father is here first. Do you want to talk with him?"

I was completely surprised. I didn't even think of connecting with Dad. I only had Dean on my mind.

Tentatively I said, "Sure? Yes."

"He is crying big tears and wants to apologize for being a poor father. For treating you and your brother and sister badly, especially your mom."

I said nothing and listened in silence as I absorbed what I already knew.

"He says he started drinking about the age of twelve and never stopped. He had a horrible childhood and did the best he could," she continued.

I still said nothing, as I felt numb to this information and just looked at En-May. There was an awkward silence because I literally had nothing to give or say to my dad at that time. All of my grief was for Dean, and En-May must have sensed that, as she moved forward very quickly.

She said, "He says you don't have to say anything, he just wanted you to know he was sorry."

I said, "Okay."

Then she said, "I'm releasing him now." And just like that, he was gone.

She closed her eyes and took two breaths. "Dean is here now," she said. I instantly became emotional.

"Oh my God, Dean! I love you! Are you okay?" I fired off questions as fast as I could speak them.

"He says he is no longer in pain. He loves you too," En-May tried to respond as quickly as I asked the questions.

I was too overwhelmed to realize she didn't say that he was happy.

"He is sitting next to you, and his hands are caressing your face." I wished so badly that I could see or feel him. I was so overwhelmed I couldn't hold back my tears.

En-May continued, "He says he led you to me so that he could communicate with you."

This confirmed my suspicion that it wasn't just coincidence that I had found her.

"He says he is sorry. It was his fault he had to leave. He went through his life review and is working on unfinished emotional lessons he did not finish in his time here. His journey on earth was complete, and he was no longer living his authentic self, so God called him home."

"His spirit and soul left his body two days before his actual body died. He floated above his body and thought, *Wow, this is kinda cool.* He could hear and feel you." She said, "He didn't want you to see him die. He says no one should have to watch their loved one take their last breath."

"I'm so sorry I couldn't save you!" I cried.

"He says you did everything and more, and he thanks you for all you did to save him. It wasn't your fault he died."

"Did he see his funeral?"

"Yes, he was there. It was beautiful, and he was amazed at how many people came. He thought the speeches were wonderful and you did a great job with the entire event. He thanks you for honoring him. He is with you most of the time, and he spoons you every night while you sleep. He stays with you and your dog, Cady, every evening and watches over to protect you both. He misses you and lives with you through your dreams."

En-May sighed. "That is beautiful," she said quietly.

"He gives you lots of hugs from behind when you are cooking in the kitchen. He says he did not do that enough when he was alive. He says he was with you in Europe. He pushed you out the door of your room, wanting you to enjoy the trip."

I knew what he was referring to, as I wallowed in my room a lot on that cruise.

"What about the signs?" I said.

"He says he likes to mess with the electric components and lights to show you he is there. Also, he was the owl that hooted the morning after he passed and likes to show his presence through falcons or eagles."

En-May had no knowledge of my experience with the owl and the eagles with Jim. This confirmed my inner knowing that it was Dean letting me know he had made it to heaven. My faith that his spirit was alive was so strong that I never stopped to question why I completely accepted everything she told me. It was as if I transitioned from being spiritually ignorant to this ultimate knowing, like waking from sleep.

"He wants you to know that he is very proud of you for keeping the company going and is sorry he left you with a mess."

I wasn't sure what mess he was talking about. At first, I thought it was about the truck I recently bought, but then I realized it was about an employee we had for several years that I had promoted within the company. He ended up quitting his job at the worst possible time, just as we were getting very busy and right before Dean died. Later I found out there were some tools missing and that he took all our customer information with him. He went to work for a competitor company. On his way out, he attempted to lure some of our skilled employees with him. He used the knowledge I had shown him and started the same work at his new job and went after our client base.

As I reflected internally on this information, En-May continued translating for Dean. "Dean said that he wasn't thinking clearly in the end because of the tumor and that he tried to bond with that person in hopes that he would help you when he was gone. He could not see that he was not who he thought he was."

I switched the subject, not wanting to waste time talking about work. "Will you be there when I die?" I asked.

"First face you will see, and he is saving you a seat," En-May said for him. She continued, "He hates that you grieve so much. It hurts to see you cry, but your journey is not done, and you are left to figure out what that is. He wants you to carry on his legacy."

I asked one last question, "The last day you spoke, you said the word 'sad.' What were you trying to tell me?"

En-May paused for a second and finally responded, "He was trying to say that he did not want to be forgotten."

I felt so sad when she explained this. Not because I knew what he was trying to say but because of WHAT he was trying to say and that he could not speak in those last days.

After our meeting was over, I felt elated. I had communicated with Dean. He was still in existence! He was okay! I would be with him again. My emotional state was a wondrous euphoria, and the whole experience felt almost surreal. How amazing to know that we do not cease to exist after death. When I thought of all the pain, fear, and sadness Dean felt before passing, I was in awe of his bravery. Then to reach out after death to reassure me of life beyond—that was the biggest gift he could have ever given me.

My feelings of happiness lasted about two days, and then I fell back into a stronger grief than before the reading. Now I knew Dean was with me, but I could not see or hear him. I started to live for the signs from him, and I still missed him more than ever. How cruel, to know that he was so close but unavailable to me in every way.

I asked En-May, "Why can he see and hear me but I can't see, touch, or feel him?"

She replied, "I can see him."

"Oh." I had to process that for a minute. I guess only certain people connect with spirits, but I wanted to be one of them.

My next medium appointment was with Lisa in July, a couple of months later. She was the first medium I had found and made an appointment with three months before. She came to my place to do my reading, as she did not have an office. Previously, she was quick to let me know in advance that Dean might not come through. Mediums can never guarantee that they can connect with spirits just because someone wants them too. But I knew if she came to my home that she would find Dean because his presence was so strong everywhere in our house. So, it was no surprise that when she first arrived, she walked in and said, "Dean is everywhere." I liked her persona; she had positive energy and was young and attractive. She did not look like a typical person who had her abilities, at least based on my preconceived ideas of what a medium looked like.

I asked her to sit down in Dean's favorite chair. I noticed that like En-May, she started by closing her eyes and taking several deep breaths. She started in immediately, saying that he was with us, and as we talked she said the love and adoration he felt for me was overwhelming and he was joking and flirting with us both.

"He is very excited and wants me to tell you that he got a Ten Point Buck."

I laughed because that was so Dean! It was just like him to burst out with pride regarding his hunting abilities.

"He says that he can do so much more there than here. He can fish and hunt and live without stress. The colors in his world are so vibrant."

There was a different vibe with this reading. I could tell Dean was coming through stronger, and his true personality shined through this medium's translation—another confirmation to me that there was life after death and that Dean was truly with me.

"He is still working on his emotional well-being from being sick and working out other issues with his life review. He says that when he was in the hospital he saw his father. His father told him that he knew he was the last person Dean wanted to see, but it was time to go."

I was very impressed by this insight. Dean's father had died some time ago, but I hadn't told her this or that Dean had a broken relationship with his father.

"He is with you at your home a lot and curls up next to you every night. He loves that you wear his T-shirts to bed."

I could only believe that what she was saying was true. How did she know I wore his T-shirts every night?

She also confirmed what En-May had said, that he slept with me every night.

I asked if he wanted me to give his daughter a message.

Lisa said, "He says that he is so proud of Karly, that he thinks she is so beautiful. He wants to apologize for his behavior when they fought the summer before his illness at a family reunion. It was his issue not hers, and he feels bad about how he acted."

He was referring to a year before his diagnosis when we hosted a family reunion at our home and Karly decided to go out of town with her boyfriend rather than attend. Dean was very hurt, especially because it was probably going to be the last time his entire family would be together. It had already been years since they had all been in one place at the same time. Dean did not speak to her for several months because of those events.

Lisa went on to say, "He says that Karly will split up with her boyfriend, Matt, and hopes that neither cheats before it happens. He doesn't want to see either one hurt."

I thought at the time that information seemed far-fetched. Karly and Matt acted more in love than ever. In fact, they had just moved in together and Karly had sold her condo. But six months later, they broke up, and Karly moved out and bought a condo on her own.

"He wants you to know that he was the owl outside your window that morning after he died and also the owl on the trail when you went running. He says to listen for a woodpecker on your next run or hike with your dog, Cady. He will be sending you a Creedence Clearwater song."

At the time, I thought that was strange. I told her, "I never listen to that kind of music. I'm not sure what songs they even play."

She started circling her arms in imitation of Tina Turner and singing "Proud Mary."

Okay, I knew that song, but I couldn't imagine hearing it on any station that I listened to.

This time, Dean brought up the funeral. His communication was so much stronger than in the last medium session, and I thought there must be something to the waiting three months most mediums insist on for a first reading. He conveyed how much he loved the ceremony and thanked me again for putting together such a perfect remembrance in his honor. He said Jim's speech was so beautiful and it really moved him. He also joked that Chad revealed his secrets in his speech, referencing a statement Dean used to make when he was kidding that "he was going out for ice cream," which was code for he was not coming back. Lisa continued to elaborate that Dean was still transitioning, and he didn't want me to be mad at him if I did not "sense" him as much in the upcoming month.

She said, "Once he fully transitions, he can come here anytime and be with you. He has free will."

As we continued to talk, Dean's personality and humor were so evident. It was amazing and wonderful, and I felt so happy that I was communicating with him.

He went on to say that he wanted to pick out the next man I would fall in love with in a couple of years after I was done grieving. I felt awkward and didn't know how to respond, but I mumbled, "Whatever. It's not his decision."

Inside I felt guilty, sad, and resentful about his comment. I did not want to hurt him by being with someone else, and I resented that he would have control over who I met. Wasn't that for me to decide when the time came? Not only was this subject painful but also very premature. Later, I realized that even after death, he knew my inner fears of being alone, and I believe he was trying to reach out to comfort me that I would eventually be in love again. I didn't want to be alone forever, but at that time, I could not imagine ever being with anyone else.

I felt this kind of limbo in my life when it came to love. I felt guilty that I didn't really want to be alone for the rest of my life but sad because I still missed Dean so much. No matter how hard I tried, I could not fast-track my grief. What I didn't realize was that I had to go through grief in the phases only set for me, and I could not control, change, or end it. It was hard to imagine I would be happy enough to accept someone new in my life again.

As all those thoughts flashed through my brain, Lisa continued to communicate with Dean and seemed to be having a full conversation with him, even laughing out loud. I felt jealous because I wanted to talk to him directly.

"What are you laughing about?" I asked her.

She said, "He is just so funny. He has so much personality. He is saying to watch for butterflies, electrical flashes on your Wi-Fi, deer visiting you. He also says to listen for woodpeckers. Oh, and he said he is working on you being able to smell him."

Deer? How would he give me a sign with deer? We lived on ten acres, and deer and elk were in our yard all the time. How would I know it was from him? Also, how would I be able to smell him? I had smelled all his clothes, hats, and shoes and I couldn't imagine how he could send me that gift.

She carried on while I was thinking to myself. "He is proud of you for keeping the business together, and he says not to worry about it until tax time next season. He knows that you will eventually want to sell the house, but don't sell it cheap—get top dollar."

I listened to this in amazement. I didn't agree with it all. At that time, I wouldn't even consider selling the house, for example. And I wondered where all this was coming from. But I was comforted when Dean said he would always be watching out for me.

I asked about the conversations that I had with him. How I felt his presence at times and his talking back to me in my head. Lisa said he absolutely was speaking with me and that I should believe it.

"His fifty-ninth birthday is coming up, and I am going to go fly-fishing with his best friend down the Yakima River. Will he be there with us?" I asked.

She said he responded, "Absolutely! He wants everyone to barbecue and put out a cold beer for him."

Lastly, as our time ran out, Lisa asked, "Why am I seeing the borealis lights? And fishing and camping?"

Astounded, I told her that I had been working on a photo book of all of Dean's slides of the time he was in Alaska and of his fishing and camping pictures over the years. I was creating a tribute of his favorite pictures for the family in a bound book. No one knew of this, as it was a surprise.

Lisa said, "He watches over your shoulder while you work on it, and he thinks it's really cool that you are creating a book in honor of his memory."

We wrapped up the session quickly, and I once again felt elated that I connected with Dean.

The next morning, I went for a run with Cady at our favorite park by the lake, and shortly after heading down the trail, a woodpecker loudly jackhammered a tree, making himself known. I smiled to myself and kept running.

SIGNS COMING TRUE

A couple of days later, I went to a concert with Karly, Matt, and my sister. We went to the Chateau Ste. Michelle Winery, where a tribute to ABBA was featured. It was a hot July night, and we had wine and dinner picnic-style on the grass, waiting for the concert to start. There was dancing and singing, and we had a great time. I thought of Dean every second and missed him unbearably.

Afterward, I dropped my sister off at her house, and I headed home. My sister lives in a very populated area of Issaquah up on Sammamish hill. I was driving up to a major intersection when, suddenly, two deer, a buck and a doe, slowly crossed the four lanes right in front of my truck. I slowed down, in awe that Dean had managed to give me the "deer" sign in a way that there was no mistaking it was from him. It was especially sweet because of the beauty of the buck, his horns covered in soft downy fur and the distinctly feminine doe trailing by his side.

A few nights later, I woke up around 2:00 a.m. I felt movement in the bedroom, and as I came fully awake, I could sense someone present.

I said sleepily, "Dean, is that you?"

I sat up and listened and looked around. I sat awake in the silence for a few minutes, and then I leaned back and rested my head on the pillows. I stared ahead, realizing once again that Dean was gone. I hated waking up. It reminded me that I was alone. Suddenly, the TV box lit up bright blue all on its own, and the lights held for around thirty seconds. Then just as silently and quickly, they faded off. I had not moved during this sign and found myself holding my breath. I whispered a thank you to Dean for visiting me, and I told him how much I loved and missed him.

Around this time, I had planned to attend the annual brain cancer walk/run. It was a 5K fundraiser that would honor those who were battling brain cancer or who had passed away from it. I made T-shirts for Karly, Matt, Brenda, and me to wear in honor of Dean. The image was a picture of him catching a steelhead fish. We had a fun time walking and reminiscing about him. We managed to raise money for the brain cancer cause. It was rewarding doing anything I could to help fight the disease.

July 24, 2016, dawned bright and sunny, and I awoke to what would have been Dean's fifty-ninth birthday. I got up early, excited to go fly-fishing with Jim. We had secured a guide to take us down the river in Dean's honor, and I was going to spread some of his ashes on the water in one of his favorite fishing holes. Afterward, we had planned a little birthday party back at my house around dinnertime.

It was a beautiful morning, and we took off over the Snoqualmie Pass to get to Ellensburg. We checked in with the guide shop and headed to the river. I fished off the front of the boat and actually caught two fish, which was saying something because I'd never caught anything fly-fishing before. Dean would have been so proud, and I hoped that he was watching me. As we came up to a good spot, I threw some of his ashes into the water after saying a few words. It was bittersweet, and I ached for Dean's presence. I thought that constantly but kept it inside.

There was a light wind coming off the river, and the trees slowly swayed on the banks. It was peaceful, and the breeze kept me at the right temperature sitting in direct sunlight. Our guide was super nice and gave me all of his attention, wanting me to have the best day. Jim was also attentive, and I felt so lucky to have such nice men with me making sure the day went well. We floated for about four hours, taking turns fishing.

We were late getting back home; I had misjudged the late-Sunday-night traffic getting over the pass. When we finally arrived home, nothing was ready. Tia and Chad had a fight and none of the food was prepared before our arrival. Brenda was already there, impatiently waiting on the couch, and I felt horrible that everything was so late. We finally got the burgers on the grill and the salads out, and everyone had dinner. Right after, we cut the cake and sang "Happy Birthday" to Dean, our eyes unfocused over each other's heads, looking at the sky. The celebration felt off.

I wanted it to be so perfect and special, but the dinner fizzled, and Tia and Chad left early. When everyone was gone and the house was quiet, I cried and cried. Every event that went by seemed like another moment that Dean's death would be forgotten. I had to learn to start living without him with every milestone that passed, but I didn't know how. I continued to struggle with his absence.

Three weeks later, I decided to clean out the garage. Dean had so much stuff; it was stacked all over the floor and in overhead bins. Mice had gotten into some of the fishing bags and made nests. It grossed me out, and I didn't want his stuff ruined. Nothing had been touched for over a year. I had opened a couple of bags when he went on that last fishing trip and hadn't closed them properly. I was dreading looking through his things, fearing it would dredge up so many feelings. Luckily, Patti, my housekeeper, came out to help me. We started sorting all the bags of equipment by camping, hunting, and fishing gear. I decided to give most everything to my sons-in-law and was trying to decide who got what. Patti called out that she found one of Dean's T-shirts, asking if I wanted it. I jumped up and grabbed it from her and shoved it in my face. It was oddly preserved in the neoprene bag and still smelled strongly of Dean. I couldn't believe it. It was a T-shirt that he had worn when we had both gone fly-fishing before he fell ill. The waterproof bag somehow perfectly preserved the smell of him—deodorant, clean skin, and leather. I was overjoyed and ran the shirt into the house to hide in my closet. I continued to smell the shirt for several weeks after that, but it slowly lost all of his scent, since it was no longer preserved in the bag.

Lisa, the second medium, had been right, I truly was able to smell him. I was amazed that the prediction came true.

Another event happened involving his scent when I went to the theater with my girlfriend. We had met up for drinks, lunch, and a movie. As we sat in the darkened theater chatting, waiting for the movie to start, I noticed the same smell from Dean's T-shirt wafting toward me. I didn't immediately realize what had happened but noticed that I was straining to inhale deeply, gravitating toward the light combination of leather, deodorant, and fresh skin. It hit me then that it was Dean's smell. I was so excited, but I didn't want to let on to my girlfriend that I smelled Dean next to me. I secretly exalted that he was next to me and loved me enough to give me the sign he was sitting beside me.

Another morning I woke up feeling sad, as usual. I walked into the kitchen to make some breakfast. I turned my cell phone on to play my tunes and turned on the song I had played over and over every day since Dean's funeral. As I started to sing and cry, the song stopped suddenly. I picked up my phone to see why the music had shut down, but instead the volume had been turned off.

I laughed, "Okay, Dean, I get it. No more crying for now."

Later that summer, I went to see En-May again. One of the topics that came up was that Dean told En-May that I was not paying attention to my driving.

"I don't know what he means," I told her.

She said, "He says that you are not aware of how you get from point A to point B. Your mind is always elsewhere."

"Hmm, yes, I can understand that. When I drive, I am always thinking about Dean and my grief and my life. The car is where I do a lot of that, and I may not be paying as close attention to the things around me. But I get to where I need to go without driving off the road," I replied.

"He says that he tries to watch over you by putting a protective bubble around your car while you are driving. It's all he can do."

"Okay, I will try to pay better attention," I said, then promptly forgot about that discussion.

When the session was over, I asked her if Dean was gone, as I hadn't heard her release him from the conversation. She told me he would not leave and to take him with me.

I laughed as I walked out the door. "Come on, baby, let's go!" I said into the air behind me.

I could hear her laughing as I walked down the hall to the lobby. After spending time with En-May, my mind tended to go over our conversations and examine every word and nuance of what was said so I could better understand things in my mind. My awareness was probably not on my driving, as usual.

Later, when I arrived home, I decided to take Cady for a walk at the lake. I changed my clothes and loaded her into the back of the truck. I had a doghouse in the bed of the pickup that she would usually run right into and lay down. On that day, she stayed outside and stood in the free space of the open pickup bed. I headed toward the lake, and on the way, I had to cross over railroad tracks on a bridge.

As I drove off the bridge and came around a wide corner of the road, I noticed a car driving past the speed limit, coming toward me at about fifty miles an hour. Suddenly, it crossed over the midline and into my lane, heading straight for me. My mind slowed down, and I watched the car, thinking surely they would see me and get back over into their own lane. As a collision seemed imminent, I cranked the steering wheel so the truck could veer as far to the right as possible. However, there was a forest with hillside that sloped into a ditch, so there was nowhere for me to pull over. I thought the other driver must be drunk or on drugs, and I absently looked into my rearview mirror to check on Cady. I saw that she was still standing outside her doghouse.

Shit! I thought, she is going to get thrown outside the bed of the truck if they run into us.

I looked up, and by now the car was aimed at hitting me square in the driver's door, since I had turned the truck to the right. Time slowed down further, and what happened so fast at the time, seemed to move in slow motion. I looked down about the time of impact, and I saw the car an inch from mine as it flew by my driver's side window, then I heard the loud sound of metal scraping on metal.

Son of a bitch! I thought. *They sideswiped my truck.*

At the time, I had no thoughts about my own personal safety—just that Cady would get hurt or Dean's truck would get damaged. By the time I could look back over my left shoulder, the car had rebounded back into its own lane and was speeding like a bat out of hell in the opposite direction.

All I saw was red. I was furious that this jackass pulled a hit and run and was going to get away with it. I drove about fifty feet ahead and pulled into a driveway on the left. The driveway sloped steeply down, and I could not maneuver the truck to get around fast enough, as it was lifted and had a horrible turning radius. As I pulled forward, then backed up, then forward again, I could see that I was on a blind corner and someone could broadside me at any minute.

Argghhh! I thought. *They are long gone.*

I put the truck in park in someone's driveway and started to get out to assess the damage when a man who lived there came running out of the garage.

I yelled, "Did you see what happened? A car drove head on in MY lane toward me and then hit me!"

"I heard the loud noise, but I was in the garage and didn't see what happened. Are you okay?" he replied.

"I am, but they sideswiped my truck—that was the loud noise you heard."

As I spoke, I lightly jogged around the pickup; the gentleman also walked around the truck as well. We both came back to the driver's side, and I looked at him in wonder. There wasn't a scratch anywhere on the truck.

How can that be? I thought.

There wasn't anything else the car could have hit, as it was practically in the middle of the two lanes.

"I can't believe there is no damage. You heard it, right?" I asked the stranger.

"Yes, I heard it for sure, but I didn't see it. It was really loud."

I thanked him for his concern and got back into the truck. I knew then that Dean, my guardian angels, God, whoever, had saved me and I had witnessed a miracle. I drove off in wonder and thanked all the spirits, including Dean, for saving my life. It would not be the last time I experienced such wonderful phenomena.

Over time, all of the predictions that the mediums had given me slowly came true. Every one of them. There was no time frame when they would happen, and some that I had doubted or forgotten about came to fruition, which helped me to believe more than ever in life after death. But even though all of those events were comforting, they did not stop the grief.

No one could fix that, only myself.

THERAPY AND GRIEF COUNSELING

I have always been proactive whenever there is a problem in my life. I am impatient with myself when something is broken, and I want to fix it right away. Since I was so depressed, I decided to go see a therapist in addition to the mediums. I also signed myself up for a grief group, a program offered by Swedish Medical and Providence Hospice Care.

My therapist was one I had seen thirteen years in the past, after my divorce from my children's father. It was a really tough time for me, and I had been severely depressed in that period of my life as well. After trying several therapists, I found Dr. D. He helped pull me out of my severe depression and codependent behavior in time for me to be emotionally healthy to meet Dean. I had been suffering anxiety and panic attacks at that time, and his counseling was invaluable. I dug Dr. D's phone number out of my contact archives and called to make an appointment.

In the meantime, I attended my first grief group session. Upon arriving at the Swedish conference room one morning in July, I awkwardly took a seat in the U-shaped circle of desks and chairs that were shoved together. The room was a boardroom of sorts, sterile with some dry erase boards on the wall and an assortment of tables and chairs. The group was a mix of men and women, and I did not have any idea what to expect. The gal running the group was very soft spoken, so I felt like I was in church and didn't want to speak too loudly. She took charge right away, and I could tell she was very kind but firm. There was a protocol to these groups, and her mission was to help each and every one of us to process our feelings and hopefully, lead us to a path of healing. She started with a quick outline of what we would be discussing for the day, while passing around a clear vase only had some water in it, and another clear vase containing different colored pebbles. We were to pick one of the rocks from the vase with pebbles and put it in the vase with water and then explain why we chose that particular color and size. I thought this was a really good way to get people to open up. It gave us something to talk about that was indirect to our feelings but gave us a reason to express our thoughts at that moment. This helped lead to further discussions to help release our sadness. We were encouraged to talk about our loved ones as well, and it felt good to talk about Dean to others who understood how I felt.

One of the most difficult emotions I wrestled with every day was that Dean was going to be forgotten. Especially to others who had not loved him like I did. Most people who have not experienced the death of a spouse or close loved one do not understand the ongoing pain of grief. I know I didn't until it happened to me. They don't know how to talk about death, and many people don't like to bring up the subject in conversation, most likely because they don't want to say the wrong thing.

That was painful to me because I wanted to talk about Dean to anyone who would listen. I LOVED talking about him. He was in my thoughts every minute of the day, and I wanted to empathize with the individuals within the group, sharing their feelings of loss and happiness about their loved ones as well. In addition, I wanted to share my life and stories about Dean in his remembrance. Unfortunately, his name did not come up amongst family and friends, and I didn't want to be one of those widows that wouldn't stop talking about her dead husband, making other people feel awkward. But, in the group, everyone would talk about their spouse that had passed, and we all understood how the others felt. It was cathartic knowing I was not alone in what I was going through.

Each person processed their grief in a different way. Some were very reserved, and others more outspoken. I was told by a couple of group attendees that they felt especially bad for me. I was particularly outspoken about my experiences of Dean's illness and struggled with breaking down emotionally a lot in front of the group. I couldn't help it; when I talked about Dean's cancer and subsequent death, more feelings welled up and bubbled out of me in slobbering tears and snot. I was embarrassed to show my emotions so openly, but I did not know how to control them and was encouraged to release those feelings anyway.

The instructor would have a different topic on grief each week. One of the assignments was to list a loss of any type that we had experienced in our lives—from losing a friend, animal, or family member to losing a home, job, or a dream. This not only helped me to understand that we suffer many losses throughout our lives, but it also showed me how to process those losses and continue moving forward.

Another group I attended later on was called the Modern Widows Club. I thoroughly enjoyed this group of women and still continue to go to meetings. There was a multitude of widows that came, young and old. How they lost a husband didn't matter—it was only important that we had all experienced the loss of our best friend, lover, and spouse in one way or another. It's a club no one wants to join, but I'm glad that I'm a part of. The first visit, I was expecting awkward mingling and trying to fit into a club where I didn't know anyone. Instead, the founder hugged me and proudly walked me into the kitchen, where everyone was sampling the assorted potluck meals. Everyone brought food of some kind, and of course, there was wine. She showed me around and personally introduced me to everyone in the room. I was pleasantly surprised to feel enveloped by the warmth and welcome of these women; it was like a big hug.

Everyone convened to the living room and sat in a big circle. One by one, we went around to introduce ourselves and, if we wanted, discuss where we were in our individual journeys. I started crying as I talked, but I didn't feel embarrassed at all. One lady quickly jumped up and sat next to me and gave me a hug. Another handed me tissues, and everyone commented on my story. It was heartwarming and helped me to realize that so many of us are living parallel lives. We all have such similar journeys in this lifetime, and none of us are really alone.

Another form of support was a woman I met on the ABTA (American Brain Tumor Association) website. We started emailing each other weekly. The fact that she was from London did not make a difference; I felt I had met a soul sister in my GBM journey. She and

I continue to correspond to this day. She, too, had lost her husband to GBM, but they were a much younger couple, only in their early thirties. We were able to talk about anything and everything. There was a familiarity in our shared pain, and both of us could talk about our loss and heartache without fear of judgment or false feelings.

As I continued to see mediums and attend local grief groups, I routinely talked with my therapist. He was always enlightening and helpful, but he could not fix my grief. I would talk about my struggle to be happy and move on with life, and about my feelings of losing my identity, but my grief did not abate after hearing his wisdom. I seemed to have better clarity and relief from En-May than he was able to give me, so eventually, I stopped his services.

Lastly, one of the things En-May encouraged me to do was get involved with volunteer work. This gave me the idea to search for donating time toward ending brain cancer. By chance one day while going through my emails, I stumbled across one of the support groups that Dean and I had attended at the UW. We had met an eighteen-year survivor of GBM, and he had emailed me one of his newsletters. I noticed he referenced a foundation called End Brain Cancer Foundation (formerly the Chris Elliott Fund, endbraincancer.org). I called their office and made an appointment to meet the founder Dellann Elliott. Upon our first interview, she and I clicked. She, too, had lost her husband to GBM around twelve years ago, and she suggested that I become a patient advocate, a position where I would support clients who came to the foundation for help. I would help with researching clinical trials, looking for local specialists near the patient's location, and choosing a different protocol better suited to the patient's needs. EBC's mission was to provide that area of support at no charge to those in need—a service clearly lacking in our current medical system.

Their goal was to help individuals newly diagnosed with brain cancer to find the best specialist, bring clinical trials closer, and ultimately survive their disease. Their ultimate goal is to end brain cancer. Since I felt so passionate about ending this illness, I was very excited to be a part of the team. I wanted others to have the knowledge that I did not have while Dean was sick. I knew how alone I felt being the sole advocate for my husband.

I also volunteered briefly at Swedish. Since they were so supportive during Dean's and my Dad's end of life, I thought it would be nice to work there. Unfortunately, it was not a good fit. As time went on, the combination of volunteering at both End Brain Cancer Foundation and Swedish became stressful as I tried to complete all the work I needed to during the week. Ultimately, End Brain Cancer seemed the better fit.

Regardless, even after doing all of the counseling, grief groups, volunteering, and work with mediums, I was still grieving harder than ever.

DATING

As life moved on without Dean, a lot of my internal issues bubbled to the surface. One of the first problems to arise was my insecurity. In my mind, being single and alone was a huge problem. I felt that I was too old to date at the age of fifty-three and that no man would want me at this stage in my life. Even though this was irrational, I found myself deeply worried about "meeting" someone else before age got the best of my appearance. Never mind that I was entirely emotionally unavailable or that my grief was still all-consuming. One thing my spiritual awakening did was force me to dig in deep and examine my life, who I was, what I wanted, and where I was going. I felt so lost without Dean, I didn't know what to do with myself. I didn't know my purpose anymore. All of my future plans were gone, and the only person who would have understood my feelings had died.

Several months after being alone, I guiltily went online and searched a couple of different dating sites. I was very discouraged once I saw available men in my age group. I looked young for my age, and I definitely acted young; and most of the men I noticed looked, well, just so old. Regardless, I went ahead and signed up to an online dating site for a month, only because I could not fully see who was on the program without doing so. Immediately, I started getting some emails from several men. My reaction to their interest was repulsion, and I should have tuned into my instinct that I was not ready to be dating.

However, my messed-up inner voice urged me forward, and I casually sifted through the emailed responses to my posted site. I did not respond to most of them, as I did not want to even start a conversation, but there were a couple of men who looked interesting, and I told myself to pick someone just to get out of the house and socialize. It wasn't like I was going to sleep with anyone, I just wanted to be in a man's company—at least, this is what I told myself. I needed to feel what I'd felt with Dean. I couldn't live without it, and I was determined to start the process of finding a replacement.

Eventually, I responded to a man who lived in a nearby town. His picture wasn't necessarily attractive to me, but he had kind eyes, and he was close by. I started email correspondence with him, and we agreed to meet not too long after.

I remember the day I was supposed to meet him at a restaurant, and I had butterflies in my stomach. I was really nervous and worried it was going to be an emotional disaster. But before we were supposed to get together, he texted and cancelled. He was downtown working and his job was running late. He asked that we meet up another day. With relief, I quickly agreed that it was fine and to let me know when he was available again. Even though I had felt relief that I no longer had to go on a blind date, I also felt a bit of disappointment. I sat down at my computer to get some work done and saw that I had a new email from an interested suitor. I quickly read his profile and tried to figure out if he was for real because his bio seemed too good to be true. He was close to my age and he looked handsome in the picture. He noted that he was a writer and he liked to be active.

I wrote back that if he wanted to meet for coffee, he should give me a call. I learned to gauge a man's interest by whether he had the balls to call me versus texting me, which I found juvenile. This man called me right away, and we made plans to meet at a local coffee and wine bar. I had replaced my original date with a new one all in one afternoon. Feeling pretty pleased with myself, I took a shower, got dressed, and put on my makeup. As I left the house, I felt a little of that old excitement of dating that I hadn't felt in years.

I was the first to arrive, so I secured a table. I nervously watched the door and studied every man who walked in to see if he was the one to match the profile. Soon, a very tall man walked in, and I stood up to let him know that I was there. When I realized for sure who he was, I walked up and gave him a hug, much to his surprise. He did not look like his picture at first, and I realized he was heavier and older than in the profile picture posted online.

I told myself to keep an open mind and put myself out there. We seemed to hit it off, but a silent alarm went off in my head when he told me his dating policy was not to pick up a check for a date, so I made sure to cover my half of the bill when he left for the bathroom, even though he offered to pay for the entire dinner. He seemed very taken with me and commented several times that he thought me adorable. He did not want the date to end, so after wine and dinner, we decided to go for a walk at a local park. While we meandered around the swimmers, picnickers, and baseball players, he reached over to hold my hand. I felt immediate distaste—it just didn't seem right, and I felt he was too forward for our first date. The only man in my life that I wanted to hold my hand was Dean. And even then, it wasn't until we had a few dates together. But I hid my feelings, not wanting to hurt this man.

Right before it was time to leave, he suddenly leaned down and kissed me. I blocked my emotions again and stood complacently. It was a chaste kiss, and it was over quickly. I noticed that he smelled good, and I wasn't totally turned off. We ended the date with a promise to get together the coming weekend. It felt good to be flattered by a man again, and I got caught up in the headiness of feeling pretty, wanted, and taken care of—something I hadn't felt since Dean became sick.

Against my better judgment, I agreed to have him over to my house that coming weekend. I felt unbearably guilty that Dean would be watching and judging me.

My date arrived on a Saturday morning with his big Golden Retriever. The first thing his dog did was run into the front yard and take a huge dump then barked his head off. Nothing irritates me more than someone who does not control their dog. Most people don't let their kids throw themselves at guests or poop in front of them or scream nonstop for attention. Why then do people let their dogs jump on, bark at, or crap on whoever or wherever they want? I swallowed my irritation and invited him in, leaving his dog in the front yard. We didn't hang out too long at my house, just long enough for me to show him around, and then we took my truck into town to have lunch. He left his dog at my house outside with Cady, which was fine with me, as long as he didn't expect to bring him with us into the restaurant.

When we arrived back home, we decided to watch a movie. I had a room that was converted to a theater room where Dean and I had wired in Bose stereo speakers and set up a big flat-screen TV and couch. It was like going to the theater, and I decided to play the movie

Deadpool, which he had never seen. He loved it, and we sat close side by side. We made out a bit during the movie, and then later he came down and helped me with some projects in my kitchen. He knew I was uncomfortable about Dean watching us, but I shoved those feelings down inside me, as I was determined not to let it influence this opportunity to forge a new relationship.

I only saw this gentleman one more time after this. He came over one evening after work. Once again, he brought his dog, who promptly took another big dump right outside the back patio French doors. We had dinner and watched a movie again. This time we carried the fooling around a little further. I absolutely hated it. I tried to hide it, and of course, he wanted to talk about it.

What was I thinking? I was so not ready for a relationship. Why did I push myself to meet someone? I had to dig deep to understand there were different levels of emotions surging up in me. First of all, no one talks about women feeling lustful after they lose a spouse. I think I was subconsciously looking for a tangible substitute for Dean's touch, feel, and smell. But once I came close to becoming intimate with another man, I realized there was no replacement for Dean, and I could not embrace anything remotely close to intimacy with someone else. I could not wait for my date to leave that evening, and I was dismayed that I found myself coming full circle in my life. It was like going back twelve years before I had met Dean. I still pushed forward with this guy, fooling myself into believing I could have a relationship with him. I continued to talk to him on the phone for a couple more days.

That man was very intense and immediately possessive. Even though I had only known him for a total of a week and seen him three times, I finally knew he was not for me. The last time I spoke with him, we got in a small argument. He was difficult and strange, and the more I talked with him, the more I realized I did not want a relationship with him. I broke it off the next morning in a text, saying I needed to spend time working out my own issues, but truthfully, I had no interest in pursuing a relationship with him. Sometimes it's easier to take the blame and let it all go. He sent over one hundred texts to my phone nonstop, trying to salvage the relationship. It got so bad I finally blocked the number. I feel like I dodged a bullet once it was all over.

Meanwhile, I received a call from the first gentleman who had initially cancelled on me. He wanted to meet for coffee again, and since I was no longer with the other guy, I agreed. The day I was supposed to meet him, he texted and cancelled again, saying dating was too hard.

Really? Why continue to call and text me then? This entire experience of dating in just a week and a half was exhausting and disheartening.

The final straw was when one other man emailed me through the dating site. He seemed like someone I would have some things in common with. I emailed him back and received this nasty reply from an individual that called me stupid and informed me that the profile was a scam. There was no way I would have known that, and I felt incredibly humiliated even though anyone could have been fooled. What was there to gain by setting up a false dating profile? I did not understand that at all. It was enough for me to cancel my subscription and shut everything down. I was done trying to date and had to reconcile myself with the reality that I might never love again.

The one positive thing that came from all that was that I was forced to look at myself more closely and acknowledge that I needed to be happy on my own before I ever met another man. I had never had that in my life, and now was as good a time as ever. I was good enough for any man, and I just had to believe it for myself. Replacing Dean with someone else to heal my grief was not the answer, at least not yet. I needed to take the time to heal, love, and find myself. I became determined that it was my path and I would embrace it without being in a relationship. So, if the time ever came along in the future, I would be ready.

LIFE WITHOUT DEAN

As life moved forward, I felt like the days and nights ran together. I decided to try some new hobbies that I'd always wanted to do but never had the time. I signed up for some art and writing classes in addition to researching volunteer work. I threw myself into house projects that needed to be finished after Dean's death as well. I became so busy during the day that I had no time to grieve. My thoughts were consumed with work, writing, art classes, and construction projects. As soon as my day wound down and I was alone, the tears flowed like water from a faucet, and I would go to bed emotionally exhausted.

Art was a nice release for my pent-up anxiety. I loved taking drawing classes, and I attempted several types to see which I liked best. Collage with acrylic paint, colored pencil, and Zentangle were the first I tried. I had never heard of Zentangle, but it quickly became my favorite. Zentangle is a methodical type of art done on cards. It can be drawn on any paper, but the original premise was to draw a repetitive design on a small card while in a form of light meditation. I would delight in creating and trying out new drawings every night.

It would take my mind off missing Dean and let my creative side flow at the same time.

I also started taking a memoir class on the weekends. I was writing this book, despite the fact I had never published anything before. I needed to learn the basics and understand how to conceptualize the book I wanted to write. The class was very informative, and I enjoyed every minute of it.

During the day, I managed to supervise the driveway asphalt paving, and a new deck with a swim spa and hot tub, being built at home. I had to purchase all the materials and have them delivered for the contractor to have on hand for the weekends. He was doing it as a side project, so it took three months for the deck to finally be built. I also contracted him to build a large outdoor playground for the grandkids and enclose a shed. I really could not afford all these projects, but I did not know at this time how much the company was going to lose by year end. Also, I felt like I needed to finish the dream Dean and I had for the house. He and I had planned all those projects before he died, and I must have felt I was finishing the legacy of his wishes.

Before I knew it, winter arrived, blowing in with a vengeance. My home, which had helped me to feel more connected to Dean, became a burden. One night, I was feeling down, sitting alone in the living room. I lay still and quiet, listening to my thoughts. Suddenly, I heard chewing noises coming from under the hall closet. I jumped up and opened the closet door. The grinding noise was unmistakable, either mice or rats. I could hear them in the walls going to town on the bones of my home. Yuck! How did they get under the house?

Since it was night, I had to wait until the next day to call an exterminator. Before he could come and investigate, I could hear them in the wall of my bedroom munching away. I pictured them splintering the wood and making tunnels just below me, soon being able to work their way into my room while I slept at night.

I missed Dean and resented his absence at the same time. Why was he not here to help me with all the outdoor problems?

Little did I know there was much more to come. The next few incidents involved winter storms that blew in one after another. Days of howling wind, snow, and rain pummeled the house. A huge tree blew down, taking a section of the new fence out as it fell across the private road that led to the rest of the neighborhood housing. As I rushed out to see what damage the tree had done, the neighbors showed up and systematically started cutting the tree up with a chainsaw. I brought the Polaris Gator (a 4wd ATV) over, and two other neighbors started helping me load the limbs, debris, and logs into the back. I would then drive the Gator filled with debris to the back of the property and unload into a pile for burning. While we were taking care of the cleanup, the wind continued to howl through the surrounding trees and chill my bones with thirty-below temperatures.

Two hours later, we had the mess cleaned up, and I was exhausted. My back and arms ached, and I felt overwhelmed and angry that Dean was not there to help me with all the work. That portion of the fence was destroyed, and I had to hire some guys to come in and repair it. I knew that my anger was irrational, but I couldn't help what I felt, and I had to channel it somewhere.

As the wind continued to blow and howl, the power would alternately go off and on. When Dean and I had built the house, we included a huge generator to run the entire house if the power was out. It had its own power panel and was very handy in our area due to the frequent power outages. One night, during the incessant windstorms, the power went off, but the generator did not kick on. I walked outside in the pitch dark, with screaming wind almost blowing me over, looking for the source of the problem, but I could not tell what was wrong. At our house, you could not see your hand in front of your face in the dark. I gave up and went back in the house, feeling defeated. I had to wait until the next day to call the generator repairman. He came just in time before another storm hit and told me it was a loose connection to the battery. This would have been a two-second fix for Dean, but for me it turned into a $500 service call.

Still, I was grateful that I had power the next day when the electricity went out yet again. Snow and freezing temperatures for all of December brought me endless troubles with the water fountains in the back and the front yard. I would look at the hot tub and swim spa that I never used and wonder what I had been thinking in spending all that money to have them installed. Even though I finished them for Dean, he never got to use them. He died before the project was finished, and now I had to pay for spa maintenance on two spas I never used and extremely high utility bills all through the winter. Right about that time, the swim spa turned green, and I had no idea how to clean them on my own, so I had to have the maintenance guy drain and refill it. That was another $400.

When Dean and I moved into our dream house, he slowly kept expanding the gardens around our house. They were his pride and joy, but I complained that I had no desire to be a landscaper and that he was going to have to maintain them on his own. He assured me that it was relaxing for him and he had no problem taking care of the gardens. A couple of years ago, we had a major renovation installed in the backyard, with patios of Roman Cobblestone, a rock waterfall, and a rustic gazebo that Dean built himself. The surrounding mounds of dark mulch were filled with all different plants, shrubs, and seasonal flowers. It was amazing and beautiful, but now I was left to maintain it all by myself.

Also during that time, I fought the moles tearing up the yard with their mounds of dirt, more mice under the house, rotting eaves where the gutters hadn't been cleaned out in two years, storm debris cleanup, flooding from the mass amount of snow and rain on the back patio, and general yard maintenance coming into the winter.

With the onset of winter and the ensuing problems, I felt like I hit a brick wall. As I cried to my daughter Tia about all the maintenance costs coming in, she said, "Mom, you don't have to stay there. Why don't you come over, and we will look at other living options?"

I drove over to her house and bought a new home being built a block away from her house that same day.

Purchasing that new house forced me to wrap my mind around finally selling and leaving my dream house I'd built with Dean. I plunged in without thinking too deeply, avoiding examining my feelings about my beloved home. Without Dean there, it no longer felt like my home. As time went on, I felt suffocated living there. I badly wanted to sell, but even though the Seattle market was hot, apparently, living in Ravensdale was not. After a few months, when the new house was built, it was time for me to move. I still had this expensive, high-maintenance home that I had to pay for, and it was incredibly stressful. Another tree went down and took out more fencing, and the snow and ice prevented prospective buyers from coming to look at the property into March.

After several months without a buyer, I felt as if I was being tested. *What is the lesson here?* I asked myself. *To suffer financial ruin?*

I was desperately trying to keep the company afloat, and now I was to have two mortgages. Didn't I get a break somewhere in this life? Why didn't I get a free pass since I lost my husband? It was hard to fight my anger, but I practiced meditation daily to release the frustration and worry of the uncertainties of my future.

LIVING THROUGH GRIEF

As time moved slowly forward, I lived each day feeling like I was going through the motions of life but secretly treading water. I lived as others expected me to, but I had no interest in my past goals or ambition for future endeavors. I worked all day, ran my errands, and exercised my dog, but my comfort came in the evenings. I worked on connecting with Dean's spirit through meditation, cards, and dreams. I watched YouTube videos of famous mediums such as James Van Praagh or Tyler Henry. I took lessons on the DailyOm or James Van Praagh's website. I read books about spirituality, mediums, and intuitivism. Now that I knew there was an afterlife, I wanted to know everything about it. I wanted to understand where I would go, who I would see, what I would do, and how it all worked.

As a young girl, I would wake up in the middle of the night and go into my parents' bedroom, seeking comfort because I would dream about dying. It would terrify me, and I would have near panic attacks just thinking about no longer existing. Cold chills would run up and down my spine, and I would do anything to distract those dark thoughts from my head. Why I thought these things at such a young age I will never know, but I could not help the thoughts that popped into my head. I was a worrier as a young girl, and I still have that trait to this day. Even as recently as two years ago, right before Dean fell ill, I would shut out anything that would make me think of death. To go from life to nothingness was just so terrifying, and I would feel this numbness flow through my limbs in response to my fears.

I was raised Catholic and had practiced this belief since early adulthood, but even though I believed in God, I couldn't wrap my head around all that religion taught. How could a loving God send you to reside in a pit of fire? I could not picture this as real and didn't really believe in hell. My thought was that being in hell was akin to a spirit that could not resolve dying. Therefore, the spirit would be stuck between their earthly life and heaven, creating a holding place where there was no peace or growth. That would be hell to me. Even as a small child, attending confession at the Catholic church felt wrong to me. How was confessing my childhood sins—which I would make up, as I was a good girl and never did bad things—to a priest, who in my eyes was just a man, the same as talking to God? Who says this man had the authority to speak for God? He could send me to hell for fighting with my brother? I could never reconcile with that way of thought.

My way of processing my grief was to stay connected to Dean in any way possible. Comfort came in the fact that he was with me in spirit and, therefore, I was not alone. Even though I could not see him, I could feel his presence. I could talk to him in my mind. That was my way to survive without him. I found solace that I would be with him again, that we would be reunited at the end of my life. That knowledge saved my sanity.

But how to bide my time until then? Life seemed to slow to a crawl when before it was speeding by. It was now taking forever to get old. I needed to figure out how to find peace and joy in what was left of my life without Dean. There was no end to my suffering without him, and trying to find my way was exhausting. There were days I just wanted to never get out of bed. I didn't want to talk with anyone or accomplish anything but survive.

Days rolled into nights and back into days. Day after day seemed the same, and I didn't see the point of it all. I was bored with life now. My thoughts were consumed with Dean: what we did at the same time of year when he was alive, trips we went on, family events we attended, and goals we were achieving together.

I had stopped cooking for months, and I ate most of my meals out when I finally did eat. I could have opened my own Panera Bakery I ate there so much. One night, I decided to make a home-cooked meal. I fixed Dean's favorite: turkey meatloaf, macaroni and cheese, and green beans. I filled a plate and set it on the kitchen bar.

I called out, "Dean, your dinner is ready!" then broke down crying.

I experienced a roller coaster of emotions on a daily basis. Right after Dean's death, I had bottles of medication still sitting on the kitchen counter. One bottle alone was worth $9,000 for the chemo that had not worked. We had not touched that last dosage. I could not bear to get rid of anything that was his. I piled all of his supplements and medications into a plastic box and moved it to the pantry. A friend disposed of the chemo for me, but the thirty to fifty other bottles are still sitting in the box in a closet to this day.

I felt so depressed that I sometimes would listen to music and picture my life as a movie montage. I was the scene at the end when the last climactic event happened and everyone is sad because the movie isn't going to have a happy ending. I would imagine myself floating above my body, looking down at myself and viewing my actions as if I were a third party and my body was someone else. I would lay on the floor and stare out a window, thinking about death and how fucked up my life had become.

Most mornings I woke up crying, my face wet with tears I didn't know that I had shed while in my sleep. I yearned for Dean's arms to surround me and comfort me. I was no longer complete; so I was restless. How would I ever be happy without all of me here? His presence in my life filled a void within me, and I felt like it would never heal. The worst part was the yearning for something that no longer existed in this world—a tangible presence I would no longer feel. It's hard to want to live without it.

I missed Dean's laughter, his warmth, his touch, his smell, and his love. I was terrified I would forget everything about him, and the constant lump in my throat that threatened more tears was exhausting.

How can I live this way until I die? I thought. What was to become of my life?

I felt like part of me was gone and the rest of me would never be happy again. It had only been eight months, but it felt like it had been one minute. Sometimes the grief was so overwhelming I felt like I was drowning. It was as if a whirling dervish of darkness surrounded me, and I was trying to escape to the top, but all I could do was look up and see light, and I was stuck. As loving as my family had been to support me, I felt isolated. There is a solitariness in deep, dark feelings that others don't understand. I know now why some commit suicide because I thought about death a lot, since I was no longer scared of it. I knew I would never take my own life, but random thoughts flitted in and out of my mind every day. I couldn't help thinking, *What if that car crossed over the medium and hit me head on?* or *What if I were to get a fatal illness?* or *What if someone breaks into my house and shoots me?*

I was not scared, as I didn't fear dying. Could I have been any more morbid? What was wrong with me? There were people with worse problems than mine. I felt ashamed of my thoughts sometimes.

When would those feelings stop? I hated that I couldn't control them. I eventually started taking antidepressants. They seemed to help at first but then came the holidays, and the tears were back. In five days, it would have been the thirteenth anniversary of the day Dean and I met. It made me so sad that we did not get a full thirteen years together, but then I thought, we could have only had five years, or two, or one year. There is never enough time with the one you love.

The morning of our anniversary, I had woken too early and had another crappy night of sleep. I got up to talk to my brother, who was staying with me, and we had some breakfast. But within an hour, I felt physically exhausted, so I decided to lie back down for a moment and close my eyes.

I immediately fell into a deep sleep and experienced a dream. I felt Dean's presence so strongly that I cried out, "You came back!" and reached my face up to kiss his lips. I thought, *Finally, I can be with him.* But as I moved toward him, I abruptly woke up as if someone had shaken me awake. The dream was so real I was disoriented and had to take a moment to understand what had just happened. When I realized it was only a dream, I felt overwhelming sadness engulf my mind and body. It had seemed so real.

The pain was intense, so I tried to focus on my breathing by taking one breath at a time. Later, when I asked En-May about it, she told me that we had crossed dimensions, that Dean and I both wanted so badly to be with each other, but that it was dangerous because sometimes you can't get back again.

I also tried meditation, but I was not very good at it. My mind bounced from one thought to another, and it was hard to relax. My thoughts gravitated to problems or regrets, and I would get agitated and become restless—not just mentally but physically.

This was just around the time I put the house up for sale. I was grieving the loss of the house already. We had such grand aspirations of living a long life in that house, and up until Dean got sick, we were living that dream. I pictured us growing old together, sitting in rocking chairs on the front porch. I knew it was just a house, but that house had a pulse. It was a living thing that Dean and I created, and it was full of memories that were made up of happiness and love. Everywhere I looked I saw and felt his presence: The beautiful hickory hardwood floors and kitchen cabinets. The unique colored concrete countertops. The grand river rock fireplace. Every picture hanging on the wall had a memory of our travels together. Our bedroom gave me the most memories of sitting for hours holding hands watching TV, laughing over some sitcom, eating in bed, or making love. We started our lives there, and now it was one more thing I had to let go unwillingly. What if I moved and couldn't feel him anymore? I was scared to be alone. Sensing that his spirit was there with me was better than nothing.

I reminded myself that a house is just a place, that it can't love me back like my family, my kids, and my grandkids always would.

They are what is important. Living near them will bring me happiness.

It's good I bought a house next door to my daughters. I knew I would feel all their love every day.

And I do. It heals me. Slowly.

TIME MOVES FORWARD

Inch by inch, I had to learn to live again. My grief continued to be strong, but instead of coming in extreme highs and lows, it evened out in intensity. I closed on my new house but was still living in the house Dean and I built. It had not sold, and the weather was clinging to its nasty ways, day in and day out. I was awed by that winter. How much worse could it get? No one wanted to buy a house that was covered under snow. Especially one that was focused on outdoor living. During that time, the elk moved in and ate all the plants, destroyed the grass, and pooped all over the Roman Cobblestone patio and breezeway. Every week, it seemed that there was something new for me to deal with and worry about.

I bounced from feeling stronger to having flashbacks that would wreck me in one breath. As I remembered the past, I mentally saw Dean in fast clips like slides in my brain, when a memory repeated a scene over and over. But as I visualized him, my mind would back up to better clarify what I was seeing, and my thoughts became elusive due to the short and choppy clips that felt so unsatisfying. The best visual reference I can give to this was a movie I once watched called *A Single Man*. The filming was different and interesting when I first watched it, but then I realized after Dean's death that it was a recreation of someone desperately trying to remember every emotional nuance and feeling of that moment.

Early one frigid February morning, I woke up to the customary silence. I lay still for a few moments as my life and all it entailed flooded back into my mind. I strained my ears to listen for Dean, who would have already been up, in the kitchen making his morning coffee. All I heard was silence. I had been sick with a cold for several days, and I stopped to feel my body, wiggling my toes and stretching carefully, checking to see if it was better or worse from the virus that had flooded it over the past few days.

I decided that I was feeling rested since I had gotten eleven hours of sleep. I slowly sat up on the edge of the bed, sensing the urgency of my dog, Cady, who needed to go out to poo and be fed. I stood up and hobbled into the living room, feeling the stiffness in my joints from my age. I leaned down to pet Cady, just like I did every morning and motioned her toward the back door. I didn't have to speak; we both knew exactly what she needed to do. I filled her bowl with dog food and opened the mudroom door. It was frozen outside, and since I hadn't bothered to put on clothes, I shivered in Dean's T-shirt and my underwear. I urged her to hurry up out the door so I could run back inside and crawl into my warm bed.

I ran and dove back under the covers, absorbing the leftover warmth from my body. I lay still again, able to just fully relax now that I had gotten that first early morning chore out of the way. I sifted through my thoughts and was bored with my propensity to focus on

Dean and his death. I no longer wanted to be sad. I couldn't help it, but I was ready to let go of the all-consuming grief that shaped my every thought. I realized that I was really alone. I could no longer hinge my happiness on Dean's spirit. I had to live for me. I had to get a grip. Every day of life was a gift from God, but I was wasting it.

Even though I was not going to feel guilty for my grief, I needed to find happiness in everyday things. If I did not know my purpose, so what? I wanted to live again. *One step at a time*, I thought. I wanted to be a light of love for everyone I met. I needed to focus on being; life would come to me.

I didn't know how I was going to do that yet, but I was finally ready to try.

MY BEAUTIFUL DAUGHTER

Sometimes it seems that as soon as we have a breakthrough, another challenge arises to test our resolve. This was true for me less than a year later, right as I was finding the courage to live again after Dean's death.

March 21, 2017, was a day of incessant rain, another gloomy, gray day in Seattle. I had finally sold my house and was getting ready to move into my new home next to my daughter Tia and her family. I had also found a property to relocate the business; it seemed things were finally coming together.

It was the one-year anniversary of the day Dean went unresponsive at Swedish Hospital—the day I had lost all hope. I had watched him die slowly over the next nine days, not by choice, but by the grace of God.

Exactly one year later, I found out that my beautiful daughter Tia had metastatic melanoma.

She was only thirty-two years old and appeared vibrant and healthy with five children under the age of ten. The week before, she'd had a routine gallbladder removal. The call was unexpected. Cancer. It's extremely rare, the surgeon said. Less than 3 percent of the time do we see melanoma in the gallbladder.

She called me. "Mom, they found cancer in my gallbladder," she cried out into the phone.

"WHAT?" I screamed, not registering the words. I went into shock.

She started to sob on the phone, and I fell to my knees on the pavement in the driveway, where I had stopped to answer the phone while moving boxes to the truck.

She explained, "The pathology came back after my surgery, and they found my gallbladder full of melanoma. They don't know if it was contained within the gallbladder or if it has spread somewhere else."

I started to cry. "Are they sure? Did they get it all out?" Again, I looked for the loopholes in this news, unable to accept that she was really sick.

She explained that was all she knew and she had to make an appointment with an oncologist. I sobbed into the cell phone, not registering that I was still on the ground outside in the light rain in my front yard.

Glenda, who was visiting, had walked out and was standing on the front porch watching me with concern, waiting to hear what was wrong.

My brain screamed, "This can't be real." How does someone survive the loss of their husband then stare down death for their daughter? Losing a child was and will always be my worst nightmare. What the fuck? Didn't I deserve a free pass somewhere in this universe? "No, no, no, no, no."

I refused to believe it.

I appealed to Dean, my spirit guides, and God. *"Please, please, take me instead,"* I chanted over and over in my head. *"Please don't take my daughter, please don't take my daughter."*

I compartmentalized the pain deep inside of me and consciously told myself Tia was going to be okay. She would find a way to survive because I could not lose her too.

I had just started to cope after the loss of Dean. My moods had evened out, and I had gone off the antidepressant. But with that latest news of Tia's illness, I felt like it was not okay to act normal. Mundane tasks made me feel guilty. I was restless and sad. How should I be? What should I do? I wanted to physically run from the thought of losing her. I wished for unconsciousness. I could not bear the pain nor fathom losing my daughter, and just the thought brought a painful pressure to my stomach and chest and big tears to my eyes. There are no words to explain the pain of a mother who must watch her child suffer through a life-threatening illness.

We waited anxiously for the many test results that Tia had to go through. The doctors started with an MRI to her brain and CAT scans to her entire body. The next day the oncologist contacted her to come in right away for an appointment.

I got the call that morning. "Mom, they want to see me this morning. That's bad news, right?"

"I don't know, honey, I'm scared. It usually means they found something. Especially due to the fact you have a scheduled meeting to review all the test results in five days."

She sniffled. "Okay, I have an appointment at ten o'clock this morning."

"Please call me as soon as you get done," I replied.

My heart just hurt for her. I could not imagine facing death and leaving five children behind. I wanted to trade places with her so badly.

I again begged God, *"Please take me instead!"*

Later that morning, I got a text. "Family meeting at 6:30 p.m. at my house."

I knew it was bad. I texted back, "Please don't make me wait."

She replied, "It's bad."

Ugghhh, I needed a miracle! Why would I choose a life path that was so hard? I could not fathom losing my little girl.

The news came in. Fifty-seven brain tumors and thirty lung tumors, all melanoma.

No matter what we do, life moves like a freight train with no brakes. As I watched my daughter express her fear and cry big tears over her prognosis, all I could do was cry with her, not knowing how to comfort someone who had been told they were going to die before their time. But unlike Dean's situation, this time I had real hope. She was going to beat it, and she was not going to die. Somehow, I just knew this to be true.

So, it began again for me. The worry, waiting, and stress. The next five days held test after test. Just as with Dean, Tia cried when they retrofitted her for the radiation mask. I heard similar comments from her like, "How did I get here?" and "I just don't want to do this."

I frantically called Dellann at End Brain Cancer Foundation, asking if she could get us a meeting with a top specialist. We recently had a guest speaker at the office from the Fred Hutchinson Cancer Research Center, and she told me she would call him to see if he knew the SCCA top melanoma specialist. While I was reaching out to anyone I knew who might help, Tia's oncologist was putting in calls to the same doctor from her end. Tia and Chad were also leaving calls and emails for the same melanoma specialist.

Finally, after the third day of testing, her oncologist was able to get ahold of a top doctor, Dr. Thompson, the leading expert in melanoma cancer at the SCCA. He told her that in her age group, she most likely had what they called a BRAF gene mutation. If she tested positive, she could receive a new treatment called targeted therapy. Targeted cancer therapy drugs block the growth of cancer by interfering with certain molecules that promote the specific type of cancer. This treatment was much less invasive than radiation with immunotherapy. He told her oncologist to delay radiation.

It was the answer to our prayers. Unfortunately, pathology was delayed and not processed correctly. Instead of starting radiation on the fourth day, she now had to wait to see if she qualified for the new treatment plan. That was a good thing in a sense, but it was torture to wait on any treatment knowing she had so many brain tumors. Mentally, this was an emotional setback for us all. We were so worried that it was spreading quickly. We hoped we would have answers the following Monday, which would have been the tenth day after initial pathology came back on her gallbladder. When that Monday came around, we all waited and prayed. Tia had posted on Facebook asking for prayers, and the responses were incredible. She had a wonderful group praying for her all morning. By that afternoon, the results came in: She qualified! What a relief.

What I had learned was typical with cancer, the setbacks just kept coming. Since they finally had the treatment planned, she was ready to start taking the drug that coming Wednesday. However, we found out insurance did not approve her medication the morning she was to start the new drug. It was another battle for her oncologist, who appealed and received approval within twenty-four hours. She amazed us all, and we were so grateful that she fought every day for Tia's care. Tia could not have had a better advocate on the inside in her fight to live. It took until that following Saturday to finally receive the medication. She quickly started that day, but by Sunday she was vomiting and fighting a migraine. With difficulty, Tia made it through the day with medication adjustments from the oncologist to help with side effects.

Finally, as side effects lessened and treatment was tweaked with drugs for the side effects, she was on her miracle plan, and all we could do was wait.

ONE YEAR

March 30th rolled around quickly. It was so hard for me to believe that it had been one year since Dean passed away. My grief had steadied enough that I was able to grow and learn spiritually. As long as I continued to think positively in my mind about my daughter going into remission, I felt I had come a long way from Spring 2016. I was stronger, steadier, and more determined. I still had my moments. The snotty gut-wrenching crying came around occasionally, especially when a memory popped into my head that would take my breath away. But that was happening less often, and I was so busy with the fallout of my life changes that I didn't have much time to dwell.

In desperation, I had emailed En-May to ask about Tia's condition. She responded that there was nothing short of a miracle in the future. She visualized Tia healthy and happy raising her five children. I can't explain my inner knowing, but this understanding calmed my internal panic, and I knew she was going to be all right. It's funny—I would have thought that the worry and grief over my daughter's illness would overshadow losing Dean. But as the extreme fear of Tia's illness abated, I went right back to missing my husband. I learned that it doesn't matter what was going on in my life, my ability to miss Dean was a constant.

The sale of my home was moving along, and I slowly started moving boxes into the new house. There was full construction being completed, destroying the brand-new clean home presented by the builder. But the changes I had made were worth it, and I knew I would love having the new millwork, closets, French doors, and paint finished before moving in rather than dealing with construction while living there.

I used the hours of packing box after box in the old home to avoid sad thoughts, but occasionally I would come across one or more items of Dean's. I would sit still for a moment to cherish a memory but then get right back up to continue working, not taking too long to dwell. I was a machine; I systematically gave away almost all the furniture and many other things in the house. I made piles of mementos for Glenda to take home after her visit and for Karly, who wanted Dean's fly tying bench, pictures, and memorabilia. I wanted a fresh start, and the new house was going to have a different vibe than the old one. It was still very hard for me to look around the house and see Dean everywhere and constantly miss him. As I moved, I worked through the grief of letting go. I would cry off and on and spend many moments packing with tears on my cheeks.

On Thursday, the anniversary of Dean's death, Karly and I decided to take the day off. We wanted to spend the entire day having a girls' day to relax and focus on our memories and honor Dean. I had decided to get a tattoo in memorial of our life together. I thought long and hard about what to get inked. Finally, I settled on hiking boot prints, large for Dean, medium for me, and Cady's four dog paws. They would travel up my arm, toward my heart. We started the day getting facials at a spa. It was relaxing and heavenly. Karly had never had one, and she enjoyed the pampering immensely.

From the spa, we headed into Bellevue and stopped for a quick lunch at Whole Foods. Then it was off to the tattoo parlor. I was nervous, as I was still trying to decide where the tattoo was going on my body. We walked into the small room, and I nervously sat up on the chair. The artist was setting up the medical paper and guns and copying the pattern I had decided on. He held the print up to my inner right arm. I had considered that particular spot so I could see it every day and remember.

My inner arm skin was soft and white, a virgin backsplash for the tattoo. He pressed the photocopy onto my right arm and somehow transferred the print to my skin so he could follow the same pattern with the ink. He started right away, and I instantly broke out in a sweat and felt the pain crash over me in waves.

"I don't think I can do this for an hour," I cried to Karly.

"If you're going to pass out or throw up, let me know," said the tattoo artist.

"Well, I'm dizzy but have not inclination to throw up." I laughed nervously.

He replied, "Well, I had a kid throw up on me a couple of weeks ago, and it wasn't pretty."

Karly and I both laughed.

"I don't know if I can do this," I said again.

Karly said, "Focus on my voice." She then started talking and telling me stories about Dean. Within the next twenty minutes, the pain became more manageable, and I continued to talk and joke with her to take my mind off the sting of the needle. As we sat there, the radio played Dean's favorite songs, "Tiny Dancer" and "Stairway to Heaven."

I said, "Dean is here with us, watching me get the tattoo. All his favorite songs are playing."

Suddenly, I was fine. The needle didn't hurt so much, and I was having fun. The tattoo was bigger than I'd planned. The artist said that if I wanted the detail, it needed to be that big. As I watched him finish up, I was skeptical that I might not have done the right thing, making it so large. But there was no turning back, and I had to learn to love it.

Karly exclaimed, "I love it!" which made me feel better.

I handed the tattoo artist a 20 percent tip, and we headed out. We shopped, had a nice dinner at a fancy restaurant, and went to the movies. Later, we went to dinner and finally headed home. It was a lovely day, and the best part was, not only did I get to talk about Dean as much as I wanted, but I knew he was with us in spirit all day.

A NEW CHAPTER

By mid-April, my life had changed dramatically. I was now living in a new home, vastly different than the one I had lived in for the last eleven years. I was purchasing another investment home out in the country to run Cedar Creek Contractors from, and I was focusing on the EBC foundation, my writing, and supporting my daughter through her treatment. As I settled into my new place, I felt more at peace and a little happier. I could look around my new home and see a blank slate. Instead of seeing my former life with Dean play out from so much happiness to so much sadness, I could now visualize a new future. I wasn't sure what that would be, but I was slowly working on it every day, whether I wanted to or not. The past two months had been brutally emotional. Saying goodbye to my old house had been deeply depressing. I hadn't realized how subtle the depression was until I noticed that I was thinking of ways to die several times a day.

As I picked up the remaining items in my sold home, I slowly walked through all the empty rooms. Reliving my life there, I sat on the floor, closed my eyes, and visualized all the events that took place in each room. Then I would open them and see the emptiness of the room and be reminded that it was all gone. I wandered outside and sat by the waterfall in the backyard. I listened to the wind, water, and birds and quietly said my last goodbyes. I was ready to move on, but it didn't mean I wouldn't miss this beautiful place that embodied Dean's spirit. Everything comes to an end, I reminded myself.

The first night in my new home, Cady would not eat or drink. I tried enticing her with sausage and bowls of ice-cold water. It took her thirty-six hours to finally drink water and eat a small amount of food. I was careful to take her on lots of jaunts around the neighborhood. It was nice having sidewalks and being able to move all around town and feel safe. We walked our ten thousand steps daily, and my body quickly started to hurt every morning from all the work I was loading onto it. After unpacking boxes and lifting and moving furniture, I could barely hobble to the bathroom each night. At times, the amount of work and effort required to move a 3,200 square foot house of furniture into a 2,500 square foot house by myself was overwhelming.

I realized that I was pushing myself physically to avoid the feelings of transition that were stirring inside of me. It was an escape to push myself to exhaustion every day. It gave me less time to think.

I continued my walk down memory lane as I unpacked all Dean's boxes I'd brought from the old home to the new house—his guns in the glass case, pictures, clothes, bathroom items, and outdoor items. I needed to find new spots for his stuff in my home that would give me warm memories instead of sadness. I intermingled our things throughout the house, and I felt pretty good that his presence was with me but in a different way.

As I settled in, I began a daily habit of taking Cady for a walk. I was trying to cheer her up; instead, I became addicted to the walks. We walked every morning or evening and sometimes twice a day all over the area. It became my outlet to de-stress. Walking was a type of meditation for me. I would think heavily about things, and it would give me clarity. During this time, the rains continued. Almost every day there was rain. It was incessant and endlessly depressing. I did not remember a wetter fall, winter, and spring in Seattle. It was hard to be happy when the weather was so ominous. Yet, even though it was always raining, I would still walk. Therefore, I felt better.

As I exercised, I realized that my grief was an ever-changing living thing—like a foreign entity inside me that would control my emotions at any time. It started out all-consuming, taking over my mind and washing over my entire physical being. It was sad, mad, scared, hopeless, and panicked. Daily, it reared its ugly head, and I could not beat it or, despite my best efforts, get rid of it. Slowly, I learned to accept its presence and realized I had to live with it. My life was changed, and grief would now always be a part of it. As time went on, I formed a relationship with it, learning how to get along so that it would not consume me. My former self fought for independence, and that was my savior. Because without fighting for my life, I would have sunk into this pit of despair, which ultimately would have stolen my will to live.

I was now at a place where I would remember the life that I had before the diagnosis. It would wash over my mind, and I would feel happiness and think fondly of those times. I would still have brief moments of extreme despair, clinging to what once was, missing it so badly. It was as if all the intense emotions I had early in my journey that had been at a constant level would morph into a few minutes, leaving me drained. Those episodes could happen at any time, and they were very real. I struggled to keep them private if it happened while I was in public.

In my mind, I had to compartmentalize my daughter's cancer and all that entailed. As with any current stress in my life, it overstimulated my brain. I could only handle so much fear, worry, and panic. My mind continued to default to grief and losing my husband. It wasn't that I was sad over his death but that I missed his everyday presence. I ached for it, yearned for it, and at times, felt physical pain that he was gone. It was a different kind of sadness. It was no longer the overwhelming grief but a new deep inner sadness that only I felt. It didn't show, and because of this, I felt even more isolated and alone, which just made me miss Dean more.

As I walked, everywhere I looked, life carried on as normal. I would see people living life, and I would think bitterly, *Those people don't have cancer. They don't know how good they have it. Why is cancer in my family and not theirs?* But that kind of thought process isolated me from the living. So, I would work on dismissing those negative feelings and try to carry on. My brain would picture all the world around me going so fast that it was a blur to the naked eye, but I felt like I was standing still, clearly outlined against the indistinguishable signs of life around me.

Those thoughts faded in time. I continued to walk and think and grow. I realized that I had made it over an entire year on my own. I had kept the business going and provided for my children's families. I had purchased a new home and remodeled and moved into it by myself. I was working on my personal growth with writing, art, and making new friends through the EBC foundation. When things got tough, I reminded myself, just like when Dean had panic attacks, that I was okay at that moment. Breathe, one breath at a time. When

I really had moments of anxiety or needed to ward off tears, I would breathe in deeply and push my breath out. Then I would tell myself what I had to be grateful for. I would list everything I could think of until I could breathe easier.

As hard as I tried, I could not control my grief, but through my spiritual growth I found comfort. I was never mad at God because I knew that this was my soul's path and I was still in school. It wasn't until I had one of the later sessions with En-May that she told me that Dean had evolved and moved to a higher spiritual level—that he was no longer as present in my life but always a name call away.

"He is a tired spirit," she said. "You have had a lot going on, but he knows you are going to be okay. He just wants you to be happy, as he is happy."

Those words reminded me that every day was a gift from God. I was here to learn my lessons, and since I was not dead yet, I needed to get on with it. Pining away for Dean and living in the past was wasting the time I had left and delaying what I was still here to learn. I continued to have my bad moments and sometimes bad days, but I realized that I had evolved and changed over the last two years and that I still had a lot of growing to do before I joined Dean one day in heaven.

My personal takeaway from all that I experienced was so simple. This revelation was not new to others, but it was new to me. I learned that we are in a temporary body in this dimension. We all choose our paths before being born to learn specific lessons in our lives, to enrich ourselves and grow spiritually. Our bodies are a temporary house, but our souls live on. All our lessons are to expand our ability to love unconditionally. We are all one on this earth. We are connected through love and energy. Dean's path was already mapped out long before I met him. He had chosen his demise on this earth, and nothing I could have done would have changed that. It was his time to go. I never had any control of his life, and in no way could I have stopped his death.

I had to experience the grief of losing my husband to understand my strengths and unconditional ability to love. I had to remember I would see him again in the not-too-distant future. By dying before me, Dean gave me the most loving gift of all. I needed to finish my lesson of growth, learn to love those in my life more than ever, treat strangers with kindness, and connect with more people. I was still learning; therefore, I was alive. Each day was a gift to be cherished and appreciated. I had to be open to learning something new.

Growth was key to gaining knowledge, and I needed to expand my energy to help others in some way. I had fifty-three years of learned behaviors to combat. I started to think twice when reacting in anger to situations. I chose words and behaviors more carefully when dealing with clients at work and family at home. I continued to donate my time at End Brain Cancer Foundation to help others in their fight for life. But most of all, I worked every day on eliminating my sadness at living life without Dean.

Even after one year, my pain was stronger than ever at my loss. But it was constantly morphing and changing into something new. It gave me purpose to be a better person. I became more empathetic, compassionate, and loving.

I consider these gifts from Dean as well. His life enriched mine in so many ways, and I will carry a piece of his soul until we are together again.

THANK YOU

Thank you so much for choosing to be on this journey with me. I am glad that you stopped by.

Please do not hesitate to connect with me if you have any questions come up about this book, or if you just want someone to chat with.

You can contact me at: http://embracinglifefromdeath.blogspot.com

I would be happy to hear from you and I enjoy connecting with readers.

Thanks again,

–Anitra

CONNECT WITH ME

Did this book tug at your heartstrings?

Do you want to hear more?

Please visit my blog to see my latest updates as I continue to learn and share how to embrace life from death.

Also, be sure to sign up on my blog to be notified of any pending book releases or updated content. By subscribing, you will be first in line for exclusive deals and future book giveaways!

What are you waiting for?

Sign up now: http://embracinglifefromdeath.blogspot.com

ABOUT THE AUTHOR

Anitra Simmons writes a raw, open and vulnerable account of her journey through what it's like to travel through terminal illness, death and a spiritual awakening. She shares the emotions and heartache felt along the way while giving hope for the future. Her mission is to bring continued awareness to Glioblastoma and help others make better choices when facing the same trials and tribulations. She continues to volunteer her time with endbraincancer.org and promote her story in hopes of someone finally finding a cure. She stays involved with the care of her daughter's ongoing battle with metastatic melanoma while running her company, Cedar Creek Contractors LLC. She lives in Buckley, WA with her dog Cady.

Made in the USA
Las Vegas, NV
07 June 2023

73080160R00131